The
Strong-Willed
Adult

The
Strong-Willed
Adult

Dennis L. Gibson

BAKER BOOK HOUSE
Grand Rapids, Michigan 49516

Copyright 1987 by
Baker Book House Company

ISBN: 0-8010-3816-2
Second printing, July 1988

Printed in the United States of America

Scripture quotations are taken from the New International Version unless
otherwise identified. Copyright 1973, 1978, 1984 International Bible Society.
Used by permission of Zondervan Bible Publishers. Scripture quotations
marked *Amplified* are taken from The Amplified Bible, © 1965 by Zondervan
Publishing House. Used with permission.

Persons identified as "clients" represent a composite of Dr. Dennis L. Gibson's
practice, and no one individual is portrayed in this book.

Much of the material in this book appeared in a previous book by the author,
now out of print: *Live, Grow and Be Free.*

"The Far Side" cartoons (pp. 39, 53, 88, 99, 133) are reprinted by permission of
Chronicle Features, San Francisco.

The cartoons "For Better or for Worse" (pp. 16, 21, 153, copyright 1984; p. 164,
copyright 1986) Universal Press Syndicate. Reprinted with permission.

To my wife,
Ruth,
who should someday
write a book titled,
*How to Live with a Strong-Willed Adult
Who Writes Books About It*

Contents

Part One

What Is a Strong-Willed Adult?

1

Strong-Willed Means Wanting Control

I slammed my ski poles into the snow and glared at my feet. My right ski rested across my left, and I could not untangle them.

This is ridiculous, I fumed. *These skis ought to do what I want them to do.* Furious, I scowled at my surroundings. I found myself alone in the north woods of Wisconsin on a wilderness seminar. My instructor had assigned me to use the cross-country skiing skills I had learned the day before to complete a seven-mile solo journey through the woods.

I *should* have done it easily. I *wanted* to do it easily. To turn around this tree in front of me, I only had to slide to the left; but I could not move my feet.

Seething, I struggled to make the skis comply. My anger resembled a child's tantrum, except that I had no audience to impress. At whom, then, was I angry?

I stopped to examine my rage. *Maybe I'm mad at myself,* I

thought. But no, I did not feel that way. I saw myself, rather, as an unfortunate victim, a sincere fellow, simply trying to fulfill an assignment and have a little pleasure and comfort in life. I resented someone or something denying me that.

Since no other human being was within earshot, and I felt angry at someone or something, only three possibilities remained: (1) I resented my instructor back at camp for not explaining everything fully, not teaching me perfectly enough; (2) I hated the skis, the woods, the snow — in short, reality for not cooperating with me, not bending to accommodate my will; (3) I raged at God, the one person always present, and the one ultimately responsible for the design of reality.

However, I felt no anger at the instructor. I remembered what she said. I had no questions for her. That left the other two options, which really merged into one.

My wish to make reality conform to my demands constituted nothing less than striving for power equivalent to God's. I set myself into rivalry with God. The way he made things did not suit my convenience. By creation, he became the author of everything; and I, a mere creature, not liking the way he wrote the script, protested his "author-ity." I, a grown man, still thought like the strong-willed child I had once been.

Childhood's Unfinished Business

Dr. James Dobson's book, The Strong-Willed Child (1978), guides parents and teachers to shape the will without breaking the spirit of a child. But what about kids like me, whose parents never read the book? Or who knew its principles but did not follow them flawlessly all the time? What becomes of the strong will in those children?

The will never harnessed in childhood remains strong

and undisciplined in the grown-up bodies of these imper-
fectly raised human beings. And since none of us ever experienced perfect upbringing in all aspects of our lives, we
all have facets of our personalities not yet disciplined. We
all, then, find ourselves to some degree, strong-willed adults.
The Bible describes us to a tee: "We all, like sheep, have
gone astray; each of us has turned to his own way" (Isa.
53:6).

By the term "strong-willed," I do not refer to lovely qualities of courage, resolve, and determination. I mean instead
the diversion of those godly character traits into such self-
centered avenues as willfulness, obstinancy, and dictatorial
discontent. I mean lacking those inner self-disciplines that
make people contented cooperators with the demands of
life.

One day, around the time of my fifth birthday, my mother
took me shopping. As we left the store, she let me buy an
ice-cream cone. I chose a single dip of grape sherbet. As we
left the store and walked half a block down the street, I
occasionally licked the sherbet halfheartedly.

Suddenly, we got halfway across a street, the light turned
red against us, and my mother increased her speed to a
brisk pace. As I followed, the sherbet blob flipped out of its
cone onto the pavement. We arrived safely at the sidewalk,
and I looked back at my now-beloved grape sherbet lying,
oh, so lovely and vulnerable in the middle of busy traffic at
Devon and Western Avenue on Chicago's North Side.

I begged my mother to let me pick it up and eat it. She
said *no*, since falling on the dirty street had made the morsel
filthy and therefore hazardous to my health. Because I
couldn't have it, I *had* to have it. As I stood on the curb
lusting for my sherbet, it glistened more beautifully in the
sun than any jewel in heaven or earth. Its flavor cried out
to me from the asphalt, sweeter, more delectable of subtle

grape nuance than any other gustatory pleasure yet savored in the collective experiences of mankind.

My mother offered to take me back to the store and buy a replacement. I insisted I had to have the one that fell on the street. Mom held firm: new sherbet or no sherbet. I accepted her offer. The clerk scooped another ball of grape sherbet from the same tub as the first one. It tasted bland, it had no color, no life, no mystique. Only the one lost to me towered in splendor over all other possible grape sherbet cones. I wanted what I did not have, and I did not want it when I had it. I glorified the unattainable.

The grape sherbet saga happened at age five. At age forty-five I sauntered into a men's clothing store and saw a black-watch plaid tie on sale at half-price. I thought how nice it would look with a blue blazer and gray slacks. On the other hand, I reasoned, I had enough ties already and could pass this one up for the sake of thrift. On the other hand, at half price. ... I debated back and forth like that with myself for several minutes.

I had recently read in Leon Salzman's classic psychology book, *The Obsessive Personality* (1968), that indecision stands tall among hallmarks of obsessive-compulsive personality disorders — a technical term for extremely strong-willed adults. Now here I saw myself doing the very thing I diagnose in my clients. I decided to put off my decision about the tie until another time. I would sleep on it, rather than rush to a hasty choice.

Several days later, I happened by the clothing store again and thought I would poke my head in and just remind myself how the tie looked. I could not find the tie! Someone else had bought it. Suddenly I *had* to have the tie. I remembered vividly the rich depth of colors in the blue-green plaid. Oh, the texture, the superb workmanship. I cursed my indecision. *You fool,* I jabbed at myself, *you don't find bargains like that every day!*

For hours later that day I could think of nothing but the lost tie. I recognized I was having a *grief* reaction! *Grief? Over a tie I did not buy?* I decided to do a little therapy on myself to understand this inappropriate emotional overreaction.

I realized I could go down the street to another clothing store and buy the same tie at full price. I did not want to. Therefore, my grief had nothing to do with the tie itself. I discovered that I mourned not the loss of the tie, or even the bargain, but the freedom to toy with whether to buy it or not.

I did not like anybody else taking my freedom of choice away from me. I preferred that reality adjust itself to my wishes. Nobody else should ever buy the tie, the merchant should keep it on half-price sale forever — all so that I would never have to make a decision nor lose the option to do so. When I realized this arrogant demand, I chuckled at myself. My depression and obsession dissolved into good humor's benign solvent.

Months later I finally did buy a black-watch tie at the regular price. I seldom wear it.

Grape sherbet for the strong-willed child. Black-watch tie for the strong-willed adult. At both ages they care little for things they have, and absolutely "need" things they don't have. They demand the power to *make* events go the way they *want* want them to go.

Cartoonist Lynn Johnston expresses this insight in her "macamoni" selection below.

Sound Familiar?

Do you recognize yourself or someone you know in the above stories? If not, read no further. You will not under-

stand this book, and it will not uplift you. You will feel like an outsider not getting the punch line of a joke that all the insiders laugh at.

But you probably will grasp this book if you are prone to depression, pessimism, perfectionism, impatience, bad temper, arguments with others, phobias, shyness, guilt feelings, persistent bad habits in your thought life, or having to have things your way.

If that list or the above stories trigger a "that's me" reaction in you, this book will help you to understand more about yourself, how you got that way, and how you can grow out of the clinging quicksand of strong-willed childhood. It will offer you new eyes with which to see God as your ultimate Father, choreographing the hardships of your day-to-day life, in order to finish the parenting that your childhood caretakers left undone. You *can* learn self-discipline at any age.

If the above examples of strong-willed adult behavior move you to say, "I know someone *else* like that," then read on. You can come to understand such persons so that you conduct yourself with poise toward them, based on compassion that steers you between the extremes of indulgence and exasperation.

However, if you find yourself determined to fix those difficult people who need this material, then read on for your own sake — you too qualify as a strong-willed adult! Why? Because you place a primary priority on achieving control over events outside your arena of responsibility.

The Many Faces of Control

Why does anyone ever obsess about anything? In order to maintain vigilance against the fate feared worse than death — humiliation. Strong-willed people show a keen allergy against inferior or disadvantaged positions.

Strong-willed adults arrange not only to keep you from seeing them as they are, warts and all, but to make you see them as they wish you to. Impression management consumes a major chunk of their time and energy.

A husband "forgets" to call his wife to say he'll arrive late for dinner. He has promised her a hundred times that he will call. He arrives home late with another empty "I'm sorry." We can translate his actions into the sentence, "I want you to think well of me even though I don't intend to change." He works at managing his wife's feelings toward him rather than his own courtesy toward her.

A woman frequently blows up at her husband and children, saying she "can't" control her temper. She means she won't. Her ability to remain calm when guests visit proves she *can* control her temper — when it suits her purpose.

Can't lives on *Won't* Street. But people who do not want to accept the consequences for directly refusing, camouflage their unwillingness with face-saving excuses or even self-accusations.

Strong-willed adults who want to change often begin taking responsibility by simply changing all their I *can'ts* to I *won't*. They begin living by a new motto for disciplined living: "Where there's a won't, there's a way!"

Other methods of opposition show more subtlety. Some people refuse to join with others, yet without appearing to refuse. We call it "shyness." Shy persons prejudge how others will respond to what they offer. For example, a man shy about asking women for dates says, in effect, "I know ahead of time that any women I ask out will surely reject my invitation. Therefore, I won't even give them a chance."

The person who will not contribute to a conversation, and uses shyness as an excuse, indirectly tells others, "I know better than you do what value you will place on what I can offer. Since I know that you will react negatively to what I offer, I will not give you the opportunity."

Such self-protection creates a sympathy-getting smoke screen. By it people defensively refuse to carry their fair share of the load in social interaction. Shall we consider shy persons un*able* to participate, or unwilling? (Where there's a won't, there's a way.)

A young Christian man anguishes in guilt, calling himself a terrible sinner for his lustful thought life. He means, "I would rather blame myself than mend my ways." He achieves a feeling of control by beating potential punishers to the punch. He punishes *himself*, thereby paying a self-imposed fine that entitles him to repeat his misbehavior.

A man jumps off a bridge into an icy river to kill himself. A police boat pulls alongside to rescue him. He refuses to get into the boat, saying he wants to die. A policeman pulls out a gun, points it at the man's head, and says, "You get into this boat, or I'll blow your brains out!" The man promptly scrambles in.

Obviously the man does not seek death itself or he would welcome the officer's bullet. He pursues the prize of control. He wants power, in this case power to make other people regret that they have not treated him better.

A strong-willed nature shows also in making demands. Demanding people insist that they *must* have what they want. They equate their preferences with necessities and inflate their "wants" into demands. What they regard as *needs* they feel entitled to as if by *rights*. They live by the notion that, because they have done or been something virtuous, as a matter of sheer justice, things should go their way and nothing adverse should happen to them.

Strong-willed persons also use complaining as a tactic to control their environment. Their language often sounds like this: "Well, how would *you* like it if ...?" But they don't really care how you would feel in the same situation. They only want to hear that you would feel so uncomfortable that you would endorse the same attitudes and actions they take. Complainers justify themselves with this unspoken idea: *If you fully realize how badly I suffer, you have to agree with my conclusions.*

A kind of childish magical thinking lies behind complaining. Complainers believe, *If I appreciate what I already have, I won't get any more. Therefore, I much prefer to talk about what I don't have than about what I do have.* Complainers use ingratitude as a way to bid for future payoffs.

We find a cousin to complaining in *belittling.* It includes ridicule, put-downs, criticism — any maneuver with which one person seeks a superior position by making another appear inferior. Notice the word *belittle* is literally a command: "B*e little,* so that I can feel big by comparison."

Similarly, sarcasm gives us subtle ways to put other persons into one-down positions. We see it easily in the cutting comments that high school kids fling at each other. They do it as a kind of jousting match, like verbal king-of-the-mountain. Like belittling, sarcasm enables the speaker to practice one-upmanship. A message of humor and hostility, sarcasm piggybacks a brilliant barb on top of a friendly gift, creating what I call a "cactus sandwich." Lynn Johnston's cartoon about compliments illustrates this unkind way to hurt someone with a put-down attached to a nourishing affirmation.

Alcoholic men often have wives who can hardly think of anything but their husbands' drinking and its effects on them. In Al-Anon, the self-help group for relatives and friends of alcoholics, these wives learn that they too have a sickness similar to alcoholism, even if they do not drink. The alco-

For Better or For Worse
By Lynn Johnston

MUNCH CLINK! MFFF CLATTER!

CAN I (MFF, GULP!) LEAVE THE TABLE, MOM?

NOW, DON'T TELL ME I NEVER NOTICE THAT YOU'VE WORKED HARD ON A MEAL.

SEE? — I JUST COMPLIMENTED YOU ON YOUR COOKING!

...NO MATTER HOW BAD IT WAS!

MMM (URP!) THAT WAS A DELICIOUS SUPPER, HONEY!

IN FACT, I USUALLY SAY WHAT A GREAT MEAL YOU'VE MADE!

I NOTICE!

holic obsesses over drinking, and so does the wife — she, too, obsesses over *his* drinking!

Preoccupation with how to gain control over what someone else does bears the unmistakable imprint of the strong-willed child at any age.

Hope for the Strong-Willed

Book after book on child raising warns that if parents fail in such and such a way, the kids will turn out awful. We adults now live in those dreaded phases of life that the books only hinted at. We inherit their predictions of awfulness in the warp and woof of our make-up and our daily behavior. Now that we have grown beyond our parents' control, who will love and discipline us? Whose authority can we learn under, now that we ourselves exercise authority over our own children?

Like runners in a relay race, we take the baton from the generation before us and acquire the job of finishing the parenting they did not do on us. We learn self-discipline by cooperating with God's ongoing fatherly love, shown by his nurturing and chastening in the events he allows in our lives.

I hated standing in the cold, snowy, north woods with my skis crossed. And so, precisely *because* I hated it, I welcomed it as a boot-camp experience in which I could become a well-disciplined soldier in Christ's army. I deliberately intensified my hatred in order to understand it better.

We often fail to taste the fullness of our highs and lows because we halfheartedly lean toward familiar middle ground. We become larger persons whenever we wholeheartedly live any event. We blunt our joy at a beautiful sunset by wondering how long the good weather will hold. I once watched that red-orange orb sink into Lake Superior as I sang alone, at the top of my lungs, with tears in my eyes, to the birches and pines and pounding surf, "How Great Thou Art." I now *know* sunsets. I *felt* that one. I took it into me. I inscribed it into my soul as a personal definition of the word *beauty*. I intensified my joy by choice.

To heartily hate my winter woods frustration, I picked up the kernel of negative emotion I felt and amplified it. "This is stupid," I protested out loud. "This is the worst thing that ever happened to me. This is the worst thing that ever happened to *anybody*. I should not have to put up with this. The universe is arranged deliberately, diabolically, maliciously, and specifically to purposely defeat, frustrate, hurt, and humiliate me."

By the time I finished that paragraph, I found myself grinning. Humor — an antidote to the grimness of strong-willed living. I amused myself by creating a caricature of what I felt and thought. And during that protest paragraph, many thoughts flashed through my mind. *The pain I felt in that Nebraska hospital bed on Easter, 1971, was a worse thing in my life than this. Compared to that, I'm actually quite well off. I'd have given anything then just to be free of pain. And to be able to stand on my feet and move around . . . what a luxury!*

When I said, "This is the worst thing that ever happened to *anybody*," I immediately thought of Christ's crucifixion. I knew that his suffering made mine a trifle. And I felt greatly encouraged to recognize that the cross of Christ jumped spontaneously to my mind as a standard by which to measure my own life. That let me know I really have seriously taken the old, old story into the unconscious, innermost wellspring of my imagination.

The smile really spread across my face when I said that the universe exists merely to thwart me. A fragment from a psalm flashed into my mind: *The heavens declare the glory of God*. What arrogance in my anger, thinking that creation exists more to aggravate me than to glorify God! I got a laugh out of that one.

This whole exaggeration process took me about half a minute. In that brief time I had vented my spleen, laughed at myself, and deepened my understanding of some key theological principles. I still did not like my awkward situation, but I *did* like something new about it: the opportunity to experience dozens more such unforgettable half-minutes ere I finished my solo.

One day in ancient Israel the prophet Isaiah came to a turning point in his life. He saw the Lord, high and lifted up — and became forever a different man. He saw with new eyes and became a new person. When we see freshly with our mind's eye, we change. Especially when we imagine God in a new way, truer to his biblical character, less like our too-small concepts of him, especially then we see ourselves in a new light, and move out of the darkness of bondage to our own strong wills.

On my frustrating ski trail, I paused for a moment to imagine God literally high and lifted up, to the level of the treetops above me. I imagined what he might feel and think, looking down upon my tantrum from tree-top level. I instantly chuckled. My antics looked comical through his eyes. I discovered a larger God than the one I experienced at ground level maliciously impeding my progress. The higher God laughs a lot. His tender, playful heart keeps him whimsical and amused, rather than grim and insulted by my tiny fits. I like a God like that, whom I cannot unsettle. I relax to realize I am not the most powerful force around.

Strong-willed adults feel secure when they let go of their own efforts to control, and instead trust God's management of their situations. Why then do they so quickly leave that security for counterfeit ones of their own design, using anger, guilt, depression, fearfulness, pessimism, and perfectionism? Oddly enough, the answer lies in two desires basic to human identity: *to be* and *to belong*.

2

To Be and to Belong

Take a coin out of your pocket. Notice that it has two sides, heads and tails. Now put it back into your pocket, and this time take out just the head side of the coin. You cannot do it; the two sides go together as one coin.

Just as you cannot separate the two sides of a coin, you cannot divide these two primary motivations in all human beings: to be and to belong. We all want to declare ourselves as individuals, and at the same time have society accept us. Not just society, but we especially want a particular group of persons to accept us — our loved ones, our reference group.

Radio astronomers recently beamed a message into outer space, announcing that we humans live here on planet Earth. As intelligent beings, we want to know what we are part of. We want to know our place. In order to know if we *belong* to a universe of others, we have to declare our *being* here, available for relationship.

The coin of human personality calls for a unity of being

and belonging, of initiating and responding. Since others call for my response to their initiatives, I recognize myself as one among many. I recognize it also by their responses to actions, like cheerful greetings, that I initiate. In this give-and-take, I experience the solidarity of belonging to a living entity larger than myself.

Not I *or* Thou

Satan loves to convince us of a lie: that we must sacrifice either our desire to belong in order to fulfill our potential; or we must abandon our identity in order to enjoy relationships. The discipline errors our parents made when we were children gave us the chance to believe Satan's lie.

Like all of us, our parents also displayed some of the strong-willed symptoms mentioned earlier. They refused, demanded, and complained — sometimes harshly, sometimes subtly. A cold shoulder, a turned-away face, the silent treatment, a scathing attack with knife-edge words — all these common forms of rejection taught us as children, "When you do what *you* want to do, you lose my love. When you do what I want you to do, you keep my love."

Of course, not everyone has experienced such harsh rejections, but it's probably safe to say that most of us have experienced them in varying degrees. To the extent we have, we mistakenly conclude: *In order to be somebody, I must be an outsider. If I want acceptance, I must be a nobody, with no ideas of my own, just a puppet who acts out the ideas of other, more powerful people.*

Yet if we isolate ourselves in the vain hope of finding ourselves, we divorce being from belonging. Since we wanted both to be and to belong as children, we soon learned to seesaw between the two positions. One time we would comply, to earn acceptance, and another time defy, to announce our own personhood. It is like shifting our hands quickly back and forth between the cold water and the hot water on a two-faucet sink, in order to come up with tolerably warm hands.

With every repetition of the seesaw, we continually set more deeply into our subconscious the mistaken belief that to assert ourselves casts us adrift from loving relationships.

We concluded long ago, in childhood decisions, that to take a stand we consider right will inevitably bring unbearable rejection from those near us who do not agree with us. So, with loaded issues, we don't wait to see if our loved ones will cut us off; we act as if they already have. We beat them to the punch we expect. We spring to the offense as our best defense. In the extreme, we act by the motto "To live I must kill."

However, Jesus said to live we must die. Die to what? Die to the lie. Die to the seesaw. Die to our mistaken childhood beliefs. Die to our tendency to isolate ourselves in order to *be* ourselves.

". . . unless a kernel of wheat falls to the ground and dies, it remains only a single seed. But if it dies, it produces many seeds" (John 12:24).

To become newer and larger than I have been, I must leave behind what I am by myself, and participate in a process which involves others. To fulfill my created potential, I must identify with, and contribute to an enterprise larger than myself. We call it *mankind, society, the group*; Jesus called it the *kingdom of God*.

The grain of wheat multiplies and grows and produces food by ceasing to exist in its individual form. It gives itself to the earth, and the earth's forces act upon it to replace its original form with an enlarged outcome inherent within it.

Losing myself raises a question, however. What do I do about my self-esteem?

A New View of Self-Esteem

Today's humanistic psychology promotes the notion that you've got to love yourself before you can do anything worthwhile for anyone else — that you've got to look out for "number one." In this theology, "number one" refers to one's self.

But biblical theology speaks of *God* as number one; and when God entered human history in the form of Jesus Christ, note his attitude. As the one person who had the *right* to demand personal exaltation, he said: "However, I am not in search of honor for Myself — I do not seek and am not aiming for My own glory . . ." (John 8:50 AMPLIFIED).

With that philosophy, Jesus passed the crucial test of mental health described in the early 1900s by Karen Horney and another famous psychologist, Alfred Adler. These two dissenters from Freudian psychoanalysis highlighted as the hallmark of neurosis the search for personal glory, honor, admiration, and superiority over others. Jesus left his exaltation in God's hands.

The Bible and sound psychology agree that we all tend to love ourselves too much already. The apostle Paul gives a prophetic list of strong-willed adult characteristics that will typify the last days. He begins the list with, "People will be lovers of themselves . . ." (2 Tim. 3:2). And today's literature in psychology and psychiatry abundantly describes the increasing malady: narcissism. In healthy living, we love our neighbors and ourselves as if members of the same body.

Writing to a different audience, in a particularly tender passage, Paul urges his beloved Philippian Christians: ". . . let each regard the others as better than and superior to himself — thinking more highly of one another than you do of yourselves. Let each of you esteem and look upon and be concerned for not [merely] his own interests, but also each for the interests of others" (Phil. 2:3, 4 AMPLIFIED).

Paul does not urge his readers to love themselves; he recognizes that they already do. He seeks to bring the human tendency toward self-love under Christian discipline. In his letter to the Ephesians, he says, ". . . He who loves his wife loves himself" (5:28). Note the order. Healthy self-love comes as a *by-product* of going out in love toward others.

The Bible calls us creatures made in the image of God. Proper worship requires us to respect the image of God wherever we find it, in ourselves *and* in others. Not I *or* thou, but I *and* thou. "Male and female created he them," perfectly designed for relating to each other. God expresses himself in the plural. He shows himself more as a tender, devoted spouse than as a rugged individualist.

To speak of a sane estimate of our own worth, let us replace the term *self-esteem* with the healthier biblical word *reverence.*

The Rudeness in False Humility

Strong-willed adults love themselves self-centeredly. They indulge false humility when they portray self-sacrifice.

Suppose you compliment me, and I reply, "Oh, pshaw, I'm not really as good as you say." My negating your statement stands a good chance of getting you to give me more. What an underhanded way of begging!

But beyond that, when I discount your appreciation, I take an arrogant stance. In effect, I say, "I am a better judge of quality than you are." I dispute your judgment. Imagine us standing together on a shore looking across the water at a flaming orange sunset. You, in breathless awe, say, "That is incredibly beautiful!" Then I frown and say, "No, on a scale of one to ten, that's only about a two."

When I throw away your compliments, I say, in effect, "By my superior knowledge, I can render a more sophisticated assessment than you can." In true humility I could say, "Thank you very much. That means a lot to me." We make ourselves vulnerable when we say, "Thank you." With that simple, heartfelt, human transaction, we let another person know, "You have deeply affected me in a way that I will not forget. I appreciate it."

But as a strong-willed adult I reason to myself, *If I accept your compliment I will be in your debt. And I dare not owe you a debt, because you might exploit your advantage over me. I dare not risk any vulnerability around a brute like you.* By rejecting your compliment, I set myself up as your judge and critic. I claim that you are not trustworthy, that you have impure motives. I will not let you affect me.

The issue behind false humility is not my acceptance of *me*, but my unwillingness to be a part of *us*. I insist on being different, special, separated out in a distinguished way. I try to *be* without also agreeing that I *belong*.

Why Do We Call Revenge "Sweet"?

What a fascination human beings have for stories of revenge. It shows not too little love for self, but too much. Our lust for vengeance offers a direct measure of our strong-willedness.

I remember a war movie I saw as a child. Humphrey Bogart was with the good guys, guarding a desert water hole. Bad-guy soldiers out there trying to get to the water treacherously shot one of our guys carrying a white flag. The audience roared its outrage. Then Bogart angrily whipped out a machine gun and went "budda-budda," right down the line of enemy soldiers — deeply satisfying the cheering theater audience.

Something in us craves the pleasure of getting back at others who have hurt us. We seek revenge for inner bruises when people treat us too lightly or leave us out. The soldiers who shot the guy with the white flag did not take seriously the sanctity of the truce. They did wrong. However, identifying myself with the good guy, I felt they violated *me*. Then I could snuff out twenty enemy lives for one of "mine," and feel myself less a killer than they.

Revenge makes a statement. If we put it into words, it goes something like this: "I want to make you feel my influence. I am going to make an impact on you because I am worthy of your time and attention. I will show the world, life, God, and everyone that they have in me a force to reckon with."

The sweetness of revenge lies in the glee of moving from a position where we felt helpless to one where we feel powerful. Our ability to inflict pain on others, even if only in our imagination, convinces us of our power and invulnerability. It gives us the satisfaction of a mission accomplished — the mission we set for ourselves in unholy vows when helplessly suffering — that we would someday balance our hurt by extracting at least as great an amount from our former tormentors.

Don't Some People Hate Themselves?

Since our problem boils down to prideful self-love rather than poor self-esteem, why do so many people have inferiority complexes? Can't we say they hate themselves?

Let us use the term "real self" for what God made in creating me in his image. This includes my capacity to change, grow, and improve. In contrast, I myself have created a glorified self to outshine everyone else and defeat all potential detractors. This glorified self includes all characteristics on my negative, old-nature side: my brittle vanity, my strong-willed striving, my childish immaturity, my undisciplined temperament.

What we call self-hate consists of the striving, glorified-self subject, I, despising the image-of-God, real-self object, *me*. For what fault? For failure to fulfill the haughty ambition of the glorified self to rise so high above others that they can never humiliate me. This constitutes my inferiority complex, an obsession with preventing any appearance of imperfection.

To serve our glorified selves, we furiously attack our less self-conscious, less vigilant, more spontaneous, *real* selves. Our attacks serve to proclaim to any observing jury how vigorously we disown, reject, and refuse to identify with the embarrassing image of God that could make us a laughing-stock. We employ self-blame to enforce the glorified self's "shoulds," which we view as the only path to glory.

We all have natural feelings of inferiority as realistic recognitions of our limitations. I cannot stop wind and rain storms by willpower. Night comes whether I want it to or not. I cannot perform an action skillfully the first time I try it; I learn only by trial and error.

Healthy, mature people use their inferiority feelings as incentives to grow and improve. Self-centering, strong-willed persons regard inferiority feelings as disasters. People who thus focus narrowly on themselves, inflating their simple inadequacies into tragedies of cosmic proportion, do not attend to the needs of society. They refuse to belong.

Hollywood movies appeal to inferiority complexes. They glorify the strong-willed adult who steps outside the rules, defies authority for a noble purpose, and prevails as an individual, operating heroically in isolation from organized fellow human beings. They give a message that feeds strong-willed self-love: "Successfully overcoming inferiority comes by individual, deviant action, and contempt for rules and order. I am the authority around here, and everybody else benefits, because I, by my own definition, am good."

To Thine Own Self Be True?

We all somewhat resemble the crazy man who could not tell Jesus his name because he lived with a legion of selves within. Well-meaning friends therefore do not help us much when they advise us, "Just be yourself." Humanistic wisdom says we must know our own minds and guide ourselves by our gut feelings. Unknowingly, I tested that philosophy one day in the woods.

I pulled my jacket tighter against the chill, as daylight began to diminish. The pine needles cracked under my hiking boots as I hurried nervously along. Night falls quickly in the woods, and I was lost. I stopped to look around. My instincts told me my car stood off there to my right. But I had walked that direction for some time already, and nothing looked familiar.

I glanced at my compass. It said I would find my car off to my left — exactly opposite of what *felt* correct to me. Certain that the compass lied, I jiggled it. It stayed steady. I jiggled it again. I wanted it to confirm what I preferred to believe. I had made up my mind and did not want any facts confusing me.

I had to choose to go either by what my feelings told me, or by the compass. I did not want to submit, but finally, by an act of rational will, against what *felt* right, I decided to obey the compass. I walked to the left and soon found my car.

"He who leans on, trusts in and is confident of his own mind and heart is a [self-confident] fool, but he who walks with skillful and godly wisdom shall be delivered" (Prov. 28:26, AMPLIFIED).

There is a way that seems right to a man,
but in the end it leads to death.

Proverbs 14:12

The strong-willed child in me had determined to go the way that seemed right, in spite of great cost. For nearly a mile I had remained "true to myself," refusing to consider any alternative. I did much better when I submitted to an authority more trustworthy than my own.

If I just let go and be myself, the self I pick might very well destroy anyone who gets in my way, including my humanistic advisors. They would quickly retract their counsel if I followed it. They would replace their advice with something more like, "Be kind to me, and find pleasure for yourself in that." That advice comes much closer to the biblical principle repeated again and again: "Love one another." That ancient, godly wisdom recognized the only path to solid self-love lies in directing love toward someone else. To be, I must belong. To belong, I must include myself by giving of myself.

Space exploration uses a principle that suggests what one can do about inordinate self-love. To reach Jupiter and the outer planets, a spacecraft from Earth must first slow down, drop out of its own orbit, and fall toward the sun. It must go the opposite direction in order to reach its destination. The sun's gravity then slings the craft into the far solar system.

So also we can reach the deep space of proper self-love when we go away from self and allow God's love first to pull us, then deliberately move us lovingly toward others. We must go the other way to get where we are headed. Thus we find our identify in the solar system of God's family.

Yet one aspect of our strong-willed nature interferes regularly with our ability to be and to belong. I refer to our powerful struggle to sit on God's throne.

3

The Right to Rule

I walked into my office one evening and hit the light switch. The lights didn't go on, though, and I became angry. I flipped the switch on and off several times — *hard*.

My action showed I believe in a power greater than my own: the electrical power supplied by our local electric company. I did not consider trying to illuminate the room by my own exertion. But at that moment, I insisted that the power greater than I must operate upon my command. My anger said I would tolerate no defiance.

Power and Pride

The Greeks called it *hubris*. We call it *pride, conceit, vanity, arrogance*. All of these imply an excessive estimate of our own worth, merit, or superiority. In the positive sense, *proud* means we recognize that we make valuable contributions which enrich the lives of others. The humble baseball hero, Lou Gehrig, called himself "proud to be a Yankee." He en-

joyed using his God-given talents as a member of a team
and treasured what the other team members added to what
he gave.

Our wrongs come in our excesses. We sin, not by using,
but by *abusing* God's gifts. We start with a seed of something
good, which God has delegated to us to use. Then we go
beyond his intention and appropriate his gifts for purposes
he never had in mind. Adding *ab* to the word *use* makes
"*ab*use." The *ab* prefix means "away from." When we make
too much of a good thing, we move away from God's purpose and make it a bad thing.

Strong will itself comes from God. Stubbornness starts
as determination, the hallmark of first-century Christian
martyrs. They *used* their determination to stay true to Christ
as Lord; they did not *ab*use it by merely defying human
authorities.

Atomic power is not necessarily bad. We can *use* it to
generate electricity and to remove cancers. We can also
*ab*use this gift from God by making bombs to destroy cities.
The strong-willed child in us resembles power not *yet* harnessed, not *yet* disciplined, not *yet* focused on constructive
uses. It runs renegade in us; not *bad*, just misdirected.

So, as strong-willed adults, we take the God-given urge
to become partakers of the divine nature (2 Peter 1:4) and
inflate it into the satanic ambition to be like the Most High
(Isa. 14:14). We thus join the original rebel in a conspiracy
of opposition against God's authority. This cosmic conflict
has no civilian bystanders. We soldier in one of two armies:
God's by conscious choice, or Satan's by unconscious default.

In rebelling, we hold an illusion of freedom. We consider
our defiance our own, original idea, when in fact we are
merely agreeing to side with the age-old delusion that our
remotest parents bought in the Garden of Eden: that a human being can displace God and take the helm (Gen. 3:5).

Cartoonist Gary Larson shows this self-destructive mutiny in his "Ocean World" cartoon.

Satan tried to seduce Jesus with the same delusion. He threw three temptations at Jesus in the wilderness. The most powerful one went something like this: "Jesus, I will give you power over everyone else if you will simply negotiate

"The herring's nothin' . . . I'm going for the whole shmeer!"

with me. Just one little act of compromise with me and it's all yours" (see Matt. 4:8, 9).

The undisciplined strong-willed child in each of us faces that same temptation. We would love to have others under our power and control. The lie that beguiles us says that we can only rest safe and content when we can finally force other people and life itself to conform to our will.

Powerless Idols

This vain striving for the throne exhausts us. Strong-willed adults long for relief. The path lies in acknowledging that the only worthy sovereign already holds the throne. Yet even then, we sometimes insist that God conform to the image we conjure up for him. We depart from the central adventure of life — seeking to *discover* God.

Heathen idol worshipers create deities as products of their own imaginations. Our idols declare how *we* see things. We then imbue those concretized perceptions with powers to function for our convenience. Yet they cannot truly function. Imagine a tribe of people living in a parched desert next to an artesian well. It would astound us if those people would dig dry wells in the desert sand, and then pant for water by these dry wells, ignoring the clear, abundant waters of the nearby natural well. Jeremiah 2:11–13 uses exactly that picture to describe the strong-willed Hebrew people seeking satisfaction in gods instead of God. We can apply the same picture to ourselves. We pursue idols of approval, possessions, prestige, and power, as if they gushed out the living water for which our souls thirst.

We always build into the gods we create a bargaining orientation. We arrange to have them torment us, with the understanding that they thereby come into our debt and must exercise their powers for our benefit. We dictate the terms of the bargain. We even decide what sacrifices will adequately appease a god and buy his favor. Overwork can hurt our health and alienate our family members. Such a sacrifice to the god Success allows us to demand the promotion, prominence, and prosperity we crave in our jobs. We find a kernel of God's truth buried within idol worship: power over us does rest outside us. The God of the Bible takes initiative out of our hands. He offers the sacrifice. He defines and refuses to be defined. He calls himself "I am." He demands the price from us.

Nearly a hundred years ago, Hudson Taylor wrote:

> How few of the Lord's people have practically recognized the truth that Christ is either "Lord of all" or He is "not Lord at all"! If we can judge God's Word, instead of being judged by it, if we can give God as much or as little as we like, then we are lords and He the indebted one, to be grateful for our dole and obliged by our compliance with His wishes. If on the other hand He is Lord, let us treat Him as such. "Why call ye me, Lord, Lord, and do not do the things which I say"? (Taylor, 1932, p. 229)

God asks of us merely obedience; that is, that we stop claiming the right to have the final decision. We not only break God's laws; we also oppose his right to rule, and demand it for ourselves. Thus we stand in contempt of court. And we hurt ourselves when we take the law into our own hands.

Power, Wisdom, and Goodness

Jesus ran into just that kind of self-demanding rebellion one day in Nazareth. The people there took offense at his wisdom and his authority, refusing to cooperate with him.

"He could not do any miracles there, except lay his hands on a few sick people and heal them" (Mark 6:5).

Jesus could do no miracles without cooperation from his needy neighbors. By their unbelief, his hometown friends had handcuffed the generosity of God. He has created us as decisional beings, who can choose to stunt our relationships. He also has created us as relational beings, who can flourish only when we join his initiatives.

Cooperation, obedience, submission — whatever name one attaches to this quality God asks of us — behind it lies an even stronger motivation: trust. Yet the strong-willed adult notoriously distrusts. I learned something of the nature of trust from another experience I had in the woods one day.

I stopped for a moment and surveyed the forest around me. The air had that freshly washed fragrance that invited me to breathe deeply. I entered a small clearing that looked like a good place for a brief rest.

Just ahead of me stood a couple of trees. I could lean against one and catch my breath. One stately old tree seemed especially inviting, but then I spotted another one closer to me. As I leaned against it, a crackling noise startled me. Suddenly I sprawled on the ground, the dead, rotten tree beneath me.

I got up, walked over to the other tree and pushed cautiously on it. Satisfied that I could trust its sturdiness, I leaned against it. It held, and my trust increased when I saw that the tree would support my weight.

Early in the twentieth century, Alexander Souter wrote a resounding definition of faith. He called faith "the leaning of the entire human personality on God in Christ Jesus in absolute trust and confidence in His power, wisdom, and goodness."

So then, by leaning our personalities on God, we say that we *know* he stands solid and strong. Yet often we reveal a different attitude. By refusing to trust God with our whole personalities, we call him unsound wood that cannot support us.

Where do we get the impression that God is *not* reliable? Nothing authoritative about God describes him that way. The Bible calls him a rock, absolutely solid, dependable, faithful, trustworthy. What authority do we then consult when we conclude not to trust God?

Answer: we set *ourselves* up as the authority we will follow. When as strong-willed adults we do not trust God, we take the attitude "I know more about God's character than anybody else does. I can rely more on my own commitment to my well-being than I can on the God who keeps my heart beating."

Power, Wisdom, and Goodness

What we believe in our hearts, revealed by our actions, contradicts what we believe in our heads, revealed by our words. We deify our feelings. We go by what *seems* right to us. We choose against the external authority of God's Word. In so doing, we question one or more of three attributes of God: his power, his wisdom, and his goodness.

Suppose I come into a situation that threatens my security, and I feel great anxiety. I know in my head that the Bible tells me in Philippians 4:6 not to be anxious about anything, but to calmly and confidently, with thanksgiving, make my requests known to God. But suppose I fret over my situation as strong-willed adults persistently do, not uttering a single thankful word to God. What am I doing?

When I doubt God's power, I am saying to myself, "My circumstances are bigger than God." J. B. Phillips wrote about this in a book called *Your God Is Too Small* (1952). The error in doubting God's power lies in considering him small and weak. I call this "ninety-seven pound weakling" theology. Philosophers used to debate whether God can create a rock too big for him to move. In doubt I say, "Yes, *my* circumstances are a rock too big for God to move. Since God is great and powerful, this probably does not happen with other people, but my case is different." Once again in my vanity, I consider myself special.

Sometimes I doubt not God's power, but his wisdom. Then I am thinking, "God does not know my circumstances. He just doesn't realize what I'm going through. If he knew, he would certainly do something to relieve me, since he is mighty enough and loving enough. But, alas, the great God of the universe, who watches the lilies and the locusts, knows nothing about *me*." I call this the "theology of the low-IQ God." Maybe J. B. Phillips should write a second book: *Your God Is Too Dumb*.

Other times I doubt God's goodness. My line of unconscious reasoning goes, "My circumstances don't matter to God. The God who so loved the world that he gave his only begotten Son callously refuses to give me the simple solution to my problem." This theology casts God as the unmovable iceberg. Mr. Phillips could complete a trilogy with *Your God Is Too Cold*.

All three show the insolent arrogance of doubt. "My circumstances overwhelm God. God does not realize what I am suffering. God cares about others but not about me." We tend to see ourselves as broken, bruised, and all out of gas. But we do this in such a way as to make God, the heavenly Father, appear guilty of child abuse! By our loud suffering we reproach God. We proclaim him to the world as a cosmic bully.

Seldom would any of us say out loud that God has failed us. But we speak eloquently by our downcast countenances, and by the conspicuous absence of praise from our language. Our unspoken attitudes testify against God: "He has ceased to be dependable. In fact, he has singled me out for special abuse. The Almighty drops whatever else he is doing in remote parts of the universe and devotes his time and attention to making *me* miserable."

Self-pity means self-piety. We all tend toward it, and the strong-willed adult specializes in it. In self-pity we make ourselves the object of our own worship. We seek for identity and distinction by suffering. We actively keep our misery alive, for the feeling of heroism it gives us.

Actually, we seldom question God's power or wisdom. That fact shows in the way we whine at him in our prayers, "Why did this have to happen to *me*?" Our *why* expresses not a question, but a protest. We don't want an answer but an apology from God! We claim special exemption from our afflictions. We require that God *must* spare us since he *can*. When he doesn't, we conclude like the Israelites who disliked having to conquer the Promised Land under Moses, that God put them in that situation because he hated them (Deut. 1:27).

Power Struggles with Parents

Doubting God's goodness probably grows out of our experiences early in life. God allowed us to learn of his nature from imperfect examples of him. What an amazing risk God has taken by entrusting his reputation to how mothers and fathers represent him!

Many parents, lacking maturity, try to build their own self-esteem by humiliating their children. They make unkind comments like, "Quit crying, or I'll give you something to cry about." Or, "What? You want to be a doctor? Why don't you just learn your math first, you dummy?" Children from that kind of background might think that God, too, needs to make himself feel bigger by making them feel smaller.

On the other hand, we might conclude that a selfish streak in God crowds out his goodness. Maybe we had experiences with parents who put themselves first. They might have set their own convenience ahead of their responsibility to care for us. They may have missed the outstanding privilege of making upstanding adults of their strong-willed children.

We also may have decided that God feels more indifferent than caring toward us. We might believe, "He doesn't even care enough about me to pick on me. He is bored with me. He yawns when my name comes before him." That attitude could come from childhood experiences with mothers and fathers who protected themselves from the demands of parenthood, at which they feared they might fail. They may have nervously looked back over their shoulders at the imperfect authorities who criticized their every mistake.

So goes the curse of the generations, ". . . to the third and fourth generation of those who hate me" (Deut. 5:9). We all stand in that chain somewhere. But those of us who complain that life has shortchanged us reveal something about our thinking. We expect the link ahead of us in the chain to pass on no curse. Other parents may have imperfections, but we think our moms and dads owed it to us to grow up psychologically whole. We consider it our birthright! Then our parents wonder, "Hey, wait a minute. How was I supposed to get so healthy? Nobody ever showed *me* how."

Unfortunately, parents have a handicap, especially toward their first-born children. They have never done this child raising before. They do not know how to recognize perfectly what their offspring hunger for. A lot of them are still starving from what they didn't get from *their* parents.

We have all inherited some concepts contaminated by

the unloving chapters in our ancestry. So we, too, tend to pass on our parents' inaccurate conclusions about God's attributes, in addition to those conclusions we formulate for ourselves.

Like spoiled children, we tend to agree that God loves us only when he gives us what we expect and want. We overlook the fact that, since he created us, he knows better than we do what most benefits us. Our strong-willed contrary attitude says, "If it's not what I am looking for, it's not what I ought to have."

But true faith anticipates not *what* God will provide, but *that* he will provide abundantly for us beyond what we ask or think. Little-faith people limit themselves to their own imaginations of what they would enjoy.

Jesus understood this, and so he used exaggeration to convey God's eagerness to lavish his favor upon us. In Luke 11, Jesus said, in effect, "Look, you people all know how even an unrighteous person will finally give in to the nagging of someone who asks a favor, right? Therefore, if even self-centered persons will grant the request of someone whom they resent, then your Father, God, who loves you tenderly, will certainly respond to your persistent praying. You don't have to twist God's arm. He *wants* to prosper you."

But we think, "Aha, you see. The power lies in the nagging. If I can irritate God badly enough, I can more likely get what I want than if I merely trust his good will." Doubting God's willingness to favor us, we take matters into our own hands. We place more confidence in our ability to pester than in God's inclination to generosity. And we apply this erroneous thinking to other relationships as well.

We thus choose to alienate ourselves. We decide that we can get the favors we want only through extortion. By irritating others enough, we can make them grant us what we want as a payment to get rid of us. We decide to pay the price and lose the relationship, for the power to get our way.

Hebrews 11:6 says that without faith it is impossible to please God. We cannot have a friendly relationship with someone while at the same time we put distance between that person and us. To try managing God by pestering him runs opposite to trusting, appreciative interaction with him. Faith says, "I am willing to connect with you and have you rule me." Distrust says, "I prefer my lonely dictatorship over a friendship with you."

The strong-willed adult fights the exercise of God's power, thinking, "If I accept any gift from you, God, it will put me one-down. I will foolishly open the floodgates to a barrage of your domination and control. You will surely abuse me if I allow you such power. You will act no more kindly to me than my parents did when I submitted myself to them." Another, more bitter view of God as a bad parent says, "If I would accept something from you, I would by that action tell the world that you have done right by me. And I refuse to give you that satisfaction."

Actually I belong in society and in the universe because God has created me and assigned to me a place of his design. He intends that I take my place and do fully what he has equipped me to do. Yet I insist on making my own way so that my place and my security come under *my* control. I take over the Creator's job, displace the Most High, and usurp the right to rule.

Scripture squarely confronts this mutiny of the strong-willed. The apostle Paul tells us that through faith, we become forever secure in a place of loving relationship to God, the author of all relationships. This real security comes "not by works, so that no one can boast" (Eph. 2:9). It comes by God's generosity, which we can appropriate only by our trusting, cooperative response.

Power in Faith Walking

God's way calls for one step at a time. In the Lord's Prayer we request our *daily* bread; God does not equip our digestive systems to handle one magnificent meal that will last us the rest of our lives. As he provided manna daily for Israel in the wilderness, he proposes to us, "Take the wisdom and energy I offer today, and trust me to know best and to provide what you will need for tomorrow."

When I jog around our neighborhood, I feel so tired in my chest and legs that I usually think I cannot make it to the end of my run. But at any point on my route, no mattter how tired, I know I can take one more step. Maybe the Bible means something like that when it says we *walk* by faith.

The *process* of my running, not the far-off finish line, becomes my focus. Faith consists not of feeling, but of movement, action — like my step-by-step running process. It means acting on my confidence that I can take the next single step. Faith means my continuing, my enduring, my persisting.

But toward what end do I persist? What do I seek most in life? Perhaps I can get a clue from Paul, who spoke of striving like a runner: ". . . I press on to lay hold of . . . that [let us call it X] for which Christ Jesus . . . laid hold of me . . ." (Phil. 3:12, AMPLIFIED).

What is X? It certainly represents a compelling, desirable goal for sensible, strong-willed Paul to willingly pay a high price for it. It must resemble what Jesus himself pursued when, for the joy set before him, he endured the cross, scorning the shame (Heb. 12:2). Imagine that! Something meant enough to Jesus that, to attain it, he willingly endured all that we abhor most passionately: pain, rejection, ridicule, and death.

What joy did Jesus see before him on the other side of

his pain? What do we learn from the quintessential Man about the nature of our hungriest human striving, our quest, our X? The next phrase in Hebrews 12:2 tells us that Jesus has sat down at the right hand of the throne of God. There it is! We seek *most* deeply not the throne, but a place with the One who already holds the throne! We confess with Augustine, "Thou has made us for Thyself and our hearts are restless til they find their rest in Thee."

How, then, did we start striving for the throne in the first place? How in the world have we ever declared war against both God and our own deepest yearning? Let's find the *root* and the *route*.

4

Roots and Routes

Four-year-old Stanley overheard his parents discussing his father's forthcoming fishing trip. "I want to go, too, Daddy," he exclaimed.

"No, son," his father replied. "Not this time." This could have remained a simple event in which Stan learned to take *no* for an answer, but three people made too big a deal of Stan's deprivation.

Stanley himself inflated the episode by throwing a tantrum. He bellowed a protest from his wounded want.

"I said *no!*" growled Father. "You're too young. You'll never be able to sit quietly in the boat."

"Yes, I will. I'll be quiet," Stanley howled.

"No, you won't! You'll be loud and wiggly and you'll scare the fish away. You can't go!" Father was shouting by now, adding fuel to the fire because of his anger.

The more Dad berated Stanley's qualifications, the more Stanley felt justified in crying, "Foul!"

Mother complicated the matter by feeling sorry for Stanley. Peeved at Dad, she unwittingly reinforced Stanley's immature belief that an angry *no* from Dad smote him with too difficult a burden for him to bear.

"That's not fair," she told Father. "You're acting like one little boy can ruin your whole day! It wouldn't kill you to take him with you. There, now, Stanley. Mommy understands," she soothed.

She implied agreement with her son's notion that life was treating him most unfairly, and therefore he could rightfully punish the world by sulking. Years later, an adult Stanley still brandished the weapon his mother helped him learn: self-pity.

Dad could have taken Stanley fishing, thereby investing in their rapport and in Stanley's healthy self-esteem. But Stanley need not have learned self-pity, even if his father denied his wish. Some out-of-proportion reactions gave Stanley raw materials for self-pity.

First, Dad overdid the way he turned down Stanley's request to go fishing. He took a bland, ordinary event and colored it red by his anger. He marked it in Stanley's mind that being told *no* constitutes an extraordinary incident.

Second, Stanley portrayed Dad's actions as cruel and unusual punishment. He magnified a happening into a holocaust. He nominated himself for Victim of the Year.

Finally, Mom seconded Stanley's motion, and encouraged his self-pity. She scowled at Dad and looked with forlorn, furrowed brow on fragile, battered Stanley, which validated her son's notion that he *needed* what he wanted. She fed his feeling that for him not to get what he had a right to demand, represented a gross miscarriage of justice, inflicted upon him by a harsh and uncaring authority.

Fertile Soil for Weedy Roots

That early family climate enabled Stanley to develop an angry style of relating to others. He saw it work for Dad. He equated anger with power and concluded that those in authority use their size and the irresistible power of anger to make others weak, little, and manageable. Little people could only wait to grow big some day and then angrily intimidate others, as Gary Larson's metal shop cartoon depicts.

Dad showed anger to Stanley. Mom showed anger to Dad. Stanley impressed Mom by his angry tantrums. Little won-

"My project's ready for grading, Mr. Big Nose . . . Hey!
I'm talkin' to YOU, squidbrain!"

der Stanley's wife complained thirty years later that he regularly became irritable toward her when things did not go his way.

The core of Stanley's strong-willed adult mentality lies in his conviction that he can force life to meet him on his terms. Like all children, he came under the influence of his parents' decisions and behavior. The self-pity they inadvertently nourished limited the development of freedom in his life and seriously impaired his fluency in responsible living. But they merely provided the influence; Stanley, like all children, did the architecture of his own approach to life.

Children, like young scientists, experiment with different ploys, to see which ones other people will allow to work. Most kids try the helpless ploy. It works with certain people who get their sense of dignity and importance from providing help to others. A basically sociable attitude like helpfulness can become antisocial when inflated out of proportion. For one person to feel help-*full*, someone else has to act help-*less*.

A typical example of the inadequacy ploy occurs when five-year-old Sharon dawdles in trying to tie her shoelaces. "I can't get it right," she whines in a tone carefully beamed on Mother's wavelength. Mother responds indulgently with, "Oh, here. Let Mommy do it for you, sweetie."

What appears on the surface as compassion really reveals Mother's vote of no-confidence in Sharon's ability. Mother's overdone servanthood promotes in Sharon's mind the unfortunate belief that ordinary tasks far exceed her ability to master them. The hazard increases if Sharon is unusually pretty. She might get much more attention for cuteness than for capability. When Mother takes Sharon's charm as an acceptable substitute for competent action, she trains her daughter to act helpless. Then the girl grows up strong-willed and handicapped.

Now consider a common variation on the above "compassionate indulgence" theme. Suppose Mom reacts to Sharon's whining by nagging, "Oh, go ahead and do it yourself. Can't you see I'm busy?" Then Sharon dawdles some more, escalating from helpless to brainless: "Which lace do you put on top?" With that, Mom exasperatedly says, "Oh, never mind. I'll do it, dummy. I swear, sometimes I wonder if you'll ever amount to anything."

By the humiliation Sharon suffers in the second instance, she pays a small price, in her estimation, for the powerful position of making Mom do her bidding. In both examples she learns that she can *make* Mom tie her shoes. She can make Mom her slave. The same helpless gambit can appeal to Mom's pity or to Mom's impatience. Either way, Mom schools Sharon to use her strong will to put others into her service. She inadvertently teaches her daughter incompetence.

In his book *Children: the Challenge* (1964), Dr. Rudolf Dreikurs cites several examples of parents who patronize their children. One tells of a child who had a serious illness, and long afterward could tyrannize Mom into servile obedience by sobbing, "How can you be so mean to me when I've been so sick?" Another mother vowed never to cross her daughter, because the poor thing had been born out of wedlock, and Mom wanted to make it up to her.

These examples show that parents sometimes take offense at hardships that have come upon their children. They feel bitter toward fate, life, reality, circumstances — ultimately toward God. In their minds, God has unfairly allowed this child to suffer, when he should have respected the child's title to better treatment. Out of spite toward God, they try to do better than he did, to right the wrong. The child by contagion picks up the same spiteful attitude, that "the world owes me."

Yet while our parents, our childhood families, and even our culture influence us, they do not determine the early decisions we make in life. We all have our own style. My style of relating to others may resemble that of my sister, but it will not imitate it exactly.

Before we reach the age of ten, we all make decisions by which we shape our basic personality structures and which, together with parental influences, form our psychological roots. In these decisions we invest certain goals (like being right, pleasing others, or getting high grades) with energy that makes them like electromagnets toward which we move. We say to ourselves, "If I can just attain *that*, I will be okay" (meaning accepted, adored, secure, invulnerable to humiliation).

That inner sentence marks a statement of faith! By it we confess a lie in place of the truth. Our early decisions to empower certain goals to magnetize us actually authorize Satan to work in our thoughts, emotions, and actions. We activate created things into greater treasures to us than is the Creator himself. "Where your treasure is, there your heart will be also" (Matt. 6:21).

Mental Maps

While we are making these decisions and establishing our psychological roots, we are also exploring and settling the new world of life outside the womb. Therefore, we all make mental maps early in life, telling us how the world looks and where we stand in relation to other people and things. Unfortunately, our mental maps are like the delicate, yellowing one I saw recently on a souvenir shop's wall.

Explorers in the early 1700s had drawn this intriguing map of the Great Lakes region. It showed Green Bay almost as large as Lake Michigan and much to the west of it. In those days, cartographers had partial, imperfect information about shorelines and river locations, and consequently the map contained severe inaccuracies. The mapmakers had done the best they could. Early explorers and settlers certainly did better with a poor map than with no map at all. That's the way it goes with each of us. We need some way to make sense of what we experience. Just as rivers, lakes, mountains, and deserts show by marks on paper maps, our mental maps consist of beliefs, philosophies, concepts, impressions, ideas, views, conclusions, and theories. Yet because we base them on incomplete information, our mental maps contain as many ludicrous distortions as that one on the souvenir shop's wall.

Paper maps can deviate in two principal dimensions: longitude and latitude. Mental maps can err in the two dimensions of being and belonging. People often deviate on the "being" axis by believing the necessity notion: "In order to be anybody, I've *got* to have what I want to have." On the "belonging" axis, they often adhere to the heresy of entitlement: "I have a *right* to be loved, approved, and accepted by certain other persons I select."

Topographical maps indicate elevation along with north, south, east, and west. You can even find them sculptured in three dimensions, to show mountains and valleys. In our childish mental geography, we greatly magnify the matter of elevation. We emphasize who is up, who is down; who is above whom, and where do I fit. Our physical stature relative to grown-ups becomes for us a parable of our worth. Big means powerful and worth much. Small means weak and worth little.

We experience disappointments and feel inferior, as if we live in a valley compared to the mountain peaks we aspire to occupy. We want to rise, not just to level ground, but to the heights — not just to adequacy, but to superiority. We so overemphasize the up/down dimension that we diminish our attention to north/south, and east/west. How severely we thus limit our own freedom of movement. We deprive ourselves of the contentment of living on the level with our fellowman.

Losing Our Bearings

As children we particularly concern ourselves with finding a place. Mature adults view "place" as a vantage point from which to contribute to society. To a still-undisciplined child's mind, *place* implies a position of prestige society owes him or her.

Bigotry consists of seriously childish beliefs that generate such hostile statements as, "They ought to know their place." By this the bigot means, "These other people stand below me in intrinsic worth. They ought to show it by deferential actions and by granting me the priority to have things function for *my* convenience, more than for theirs."

Someone might acknowledge both Pike's Peak and Death Valley as two different wonders to behold, but then wrongly rate Pike's Peak "better" because it rises higher. Jesus attacked the mistake of comparing people on a scale of value in a story he told.

An employer hired a number of farmhands to labor in his fields under the hot sun for many hours. They agreed on a fair contract for a full day's wage. Later that same day, he hired another group of men, saying he would pay them fairly. These worked only one hour instead of the full day that the first ones worked, but the employer generously paid them all the same.

The first group argued that they should have received more than the newcomers. They took as their standard of fair pay *not* what they had contracted for with the employer, but what *other* people received from him. They mistakenly compared their money not with what *they* had the day before, but with what they saw others get. Here lies the heart of jealousy: comparing our fortunes with the fortunes of others.

Why do some people persist in such self-defeating behavior? Perhaps the motto, "The prize is worth the price" can help us understand.

A woman (whom we will call Louise) demands unqualified, constant approval from her loved ones. The fact that she demands it proves that she does not expect to get it. More than approval, she seeks the prize of predictability. Louise regularly pays the price of painful rejection in order to prove that her mental map works. When she finally receives a blast of annoyance from her badgered husband, she can say to herself, *See, my map was right! Anytime I try to ascend the Mountain of Approval, others put me down into the Valley of Rejection.* Completing the vicious circle that typifies all compulsions, Louise concludes irrationally, *Therefore, I've got to redouble my efforts to get people to approve of me.*

Louise's mistaken thinking contains a partial truth. While her effort to manipulate others does upset them toward her, increasing her manipulation does not improve her situation.

Heresies generally represent not utter falsehoods, but truths out of balance. We enlarge half-truths into mockeries of the whole truth. Green Bay really does exist off the western edge of Lake Michigan — but, not like on the early French explorer's map, as big as Lake Michigan. Truth out of proportion is not as aptly called "untrue" as it is "misleading." That offers the key point about our childhood mental maps: they mislead us in our adult walk.

How We Made Our Maps

Basically out of an unbalanced diet of nurture and admonition, not suited to the needs of our particular inborn temperaments, as children we developed grotesque irregularities in our mental maps. In a nutshell, our psychological cartography developed like this:

1. As impressionable newcomers to the human landscape, we needed to make sense of life.
2. We set for ourselves an idealized self as our goal, and charted a course to get there. Our journey could never succeed because our Shangri-la destination existed nowhere in reality, but only on our mental maps.
3. Our parents followed the best maps they found, but because those maps contained errors, our parents made mistakes in raising us.
4. We distorted what we saw, through lenses warped by the stresses that parental mistakes put upon us.
5. Though we did the best we knew how under the circumstances, we could not avoid coming to mistaken conclusions.
6. We are all living by archaic mental maps, which result from our own participation in the fallen human condition. We can do with these maps of ours as we choose. We can regard them as the finest finished products possible for us ever to achieve, or we can view them as working rough drafts for improved later editions.

Strong-willed adults have love affairs with their first mental maps. They act like proud Great Lakes tourists who buy the map on the souvenir shop wall, and then drive according to it, saying, "If it was good enough for Père Marquette, it's good enough for me!"

Now note some good news: the map is not the territory! No map can ever duplicate exactly the ground it symbolizes. Since we cannot carry an acre of real estate in a pocket, we make models of it small enough for us to use. That means we have to scale down from reality to representation. Therefore, no map can ever offer us anything but a distortion. We can no longer refer to maps as "true," but as "relatively useful" for the journey we have in mind.

Rerouting

Even the best mental maps by which mature adults live distort reality. Making mature maps from childish charts requires reducing big mistakes into little ones. Twentieth-century maps *more nearly* represent the Great Lakes than did the primitive ones two hundred years ago. We run less risk of getting lost following an up-to-date map than if we limit ourselves to one from long ago.

We need not discard our old maps as utterly worthless. They do enable us to get around reasonably well. However, we have more available to us than when we stick slavishly to obsolete editions. They can serve as starting points for improved maps! Everything we can do, following an old map, we can do less painfully with a new one.

Now as a strong-willed adult, I would rather bully reality into bending itself to fit my theory than revise my theory to fit reality. Why? Because to revise my theory would require me to regard it as wrong and imperfect. That would reflect on me as an inadequate, inferior person — an image of myself which I will not tolerate.

What a burden to fight reality! Jesus said to Saul of Tarsus, a strong-willed adult, ... "It is hard for you to kick against the goads" (Acts 26:14). And Jesus said that his burden, the yoke of reality, weighs light compared to our self-imposed tonnage. What a relief to regard my original theory not as "wrong," but as "partially true, and capable of expansion in the future"!

So, I face an internal struggle. On the one hand, as a strong-willed adult, I want to follow my old, familiar map. On the other hand, as a mature, reasonable adult, I want to develop a better one. Where did this dichotomy originate — and what can I do about it?

Part Two

How Can They Change?

5

Freedom Through Surrender

Every few years in the 1960s and 70s, a news article appeared about some Japanese soldier, on a remote island in the Pacific Ocean, still fighting World War II. When captured, he learned that Japan had lost the war but had rebuilt into a new time of peace and prosperity. That heritage then became his, as he laid down his arms. Surrender freed him from the bondage of battle. He remained a fugitive only as long as *he* kept the war going.

Rebellion Imprisons Us

That same principle holds true in our relationships with others and with God. As we cooperate with him, we free ourselves from bondage to our own strong-willed self-determination. This happens when we surrender to the freedom he makes available to us.

65

A young man we'll call Gary learned this principle through counseling.

From as far back as he could remember, Gary had heard his parents say "Gary's going to be a doctor, just like his father." Gary hated the thought of becoming a doctor, since his parents had pushed it down his throat. Yet when he took high school aptitude and interests tests, the results showed him highly qualified and motivated for a medical career.

When he entered college and had to choose a major, Gary resolved not to pick premedicine. A counselor helped him to see that he was making himself a prisoner. Defying his parents' wishes gave him an illusion of freedom. At the same time, it blinded him to the fact that he was enslaving himself in his own rebellion. By his strong-willed logic, he couldn't do what he wanted to do, if his parents also wanted him to do it.

To be an individual, he reasoned unconsciously, *I must* not *do what Mom and Dad tell me to do.* He ruled out a large area of freedom for himself, by holding on to the notion that to go into medicine would mean giving in to Mom and Dad as their little puppet.

The counselor suggested a way for Gary to step out of the prison of his own thinking. With a twinkle in his eye, Gary went home to his parents and said, "Folks, I want you to know I have decided to go to medical school, even though you want me to."

A simple change in wording freed him — from *because* to *even though* his parents wanted him to. He had stuck himself on a point of pride when he could see no way for him to become a doctor without it looking like he was doing so *because* his parents commanded him to.

We might say that God kind of beckoned Gary to an adult level by saying something like this: "Okay, Gary. Your mom and dad have finished their job with you. Their wishes are now irrelevant to *your* choices. I have something in mind for you to do. In fact, I even knew what I was doing in all those events that you regarded as my blunders back there in your childhood. I assigned you to the particular parents I did to groom you for a particular use I have in mind. I know you don't like my methods, but I can live with that. I designed you to enjoy serving me as a doctor. Now let's get on with it."

All our qualities come ultimately from God. He gives them to us to use in his program of wooing the world to himself. He is looking for recruits. He created each of us able to choose whether to join him or jilt him. He makes us able to respond; that's the meaning of "responsible." We can respond *yes* to his invitation, and use his gifts in his service, or we can say *no*, and abuse his gifts for our own, self-centered purposes.

We do God's will only by choosing so, even if our parents want us to. "I have decided, Mom and Dad, that I am going to live a committed Christian life, and attend the church you attend, even though you have been nagging me all these years to do so." That responsible declaration of independence could free many young adult and teenage rebels from the prison of pride into the delight of discipleship.

Worship Establishes Us

Choose this day whom you will serve. You do not serve Mom and Dad when you decide to go to *their* church on God's orders. You do not capitulate to Mom and Dad, but surrender to Almighty God. You commit an act of worship, responding to God's love.

Our hardness to God's love call indicates what worth we place on God. Note what placing worth on God means. It means worship — attributing worth-ship to him. We choose whether to make God worth more to us, or worth less than the substitutes for him that we have discovered.

The choice we make about God's worth to us has much to do with what kind of parental personality we attribute to him. We take our distorted, prejudiced views of ungodly human authority figures and mistakenly make those our picture of God. Psychologists call this process "transference." We transfer our opinions and feelings about one authority figure to another, as if the two were identical persons. Our doubts about God's power, wisdom, and goodness represent just such a case of mistaken identity. We need not continue to make such a mistake if we acquaint ourselves more deeply and thoroughly with God's worth-ship.

How can we know who God really is and what he really is like? We can begin by identifying the mistaken concepts we hold about him, concepts that have misguided our thinking until now. We often confuse ourselves particularly about God's approach to discipline.

Discipline Develops Us

When we do something contrary to God's laws, how does it affect him? Our mistaken idea of God assumes that our offenses annoy him. Scripture teaches that they *grieve* him (Eph. 4:30). Grief implies that God feels painfully afflicted by the temporary loss of a cherished fellowship, which we have broken by our misdeed.

We learn in 1 John 1:9 that, no matter what we do, God is faithful and just in his response to us. He remains true to his own nature and promises. That is, God himself adheres to a preset standard. He does not deal with us according to his whim or his momentary inconvenience, or his irritation with what we have done. He stays faithful to something that he has, in a sense, made higher than himself: his word, his promise, his salvation covenant with us.

This covenant has two phases. In the first, we accept God's gracious offer of a place in his family. We agree for him to adopt us as his children and that we live under his authority. That contract becomes a secure fence within which we romp and exercise. It arches over us like an umbrella, larger than any event that takes place under it.

This umbrellalike contract allows us then to enter into the second phase of the covenant, the process of God's refining and disciplining us. Here we kick and scream and disobey, and God disciplines us. We have an understanding that he will never take us seriously when we say we don't want the relationship with him. We are free to have our tantrums because the umbrella, the container created by phase one, holds secure. We belong to God's family by phase one. He grooms us continually into respectable family members by phase two.

Jesus revealed what kind of parent he found in the one he called *Father*. His view shows in the fatherlike offer he made to those who considered following him: "Take My yoke upon you. . . . For My yoke is wholesome (useful, good) — not harsh, hard, sharp, or pressing, but comfortable, gracious and pleasant; and My burden is light and easy to be borne" (Matt. 11:29, 30 AMPLIFIED).

The Master struck a correct psychological balance between no discipline or harsh discipline, between spoiling or suppressing a child. Both of these lead to inferiority feelings against which children stiffen their strong wills long into adulthood. But Jesus compliments his children by entrusting them with meaningful work to do (a yoke), and making sure that it falls well within their ability to do it.

The feelings of failure and inferiority which we experience with the mind of Christ differ from those we experience with the mind of self. We see them not as disasters, nor as God having given up on us, but we see them as loving spanks from our heavenly Father, who says, "I see much that you can do. I have a place and a use in mind for you. I invested part of myself in you when I created you. I made you capable of more than you have already attained. Now quit moping and get on with it."

The sour, negative, strong-willed child in me tends to look upon the place set for me and resent it. "This is your place," to my rebellious ears means that some self-centered authority has ordained for me a rigid, frozen location where I *must* sit. The eyes of my new nature see that my Father makes freely available to me one of many possible places. My outlook depends on how I read his intentions. My old nature maintains that the authority wants to bind, restrict, trap, and imprison me. With my new nature, I know my Father wants to welcome, provide for, enjoy, nourish, and bring pleasure to me.

We need both the nurture *and* admonition of the Lord to civilize a human child. Nurture develops the "be"; admonition develops the "belong."

With nurture alone, I could develop the mistaken idea that I am the *only* important person. I may conclude that I alone initiate, and that all other persons exist merely to respond to me. I would then view my will as supreme, and have no question but that I rightfully rule the universe.

With admonition alone, I could mistakenly conclude that only other people are important. I may decide that I can be somebody only by annoying all these other important people. Better a nuisance than a nobody. Too much emphasis on admonition may stir in me the belief that others do not consider me capable of contributing anything from my own creativity.

So, God balances nurture and admonition. He disciplines like a coach who makes an athlete strain to develop the full potential of each muscle. Go out to any athletic practice ground — football, soccer, basketball — and you will hear the players complaining, "Oh, coach, can't we quit a little earlier today?" The coach says, "Two more laps." At that moment, the players *hate* it. They say, "It's not fair! This guy is not human! He's brutal!" But when the season ends, they say, "Boy, I'm glad he never let us off easy!" They rejoice because they have developed.

In Hebrews 12 the writer speaks tenderly of God as a Father chastening us. The writer knows how chastening can affect each of us because he says, "No discipline at the time seems pleasant ..." (v. 11). But in the long run, when we recognize the loving hand behind the pain, when we see the growth that we have experienced, we praise him.

Appreciation Develops Relationships

The great devotional writer, Oswald Chambers, once wrote that we often focus more on God's blessings than on God himself. We act like self-centered children on Christmas morning, who ravenously open their gifts, loving them more than they do the giver. What goes through the mind of a loving father thus ignored and treated like a vending machine?

He cares for the child and creatively plans how to jolt or maneuver the child's distorted thinking into a desirable, appreciative, and cooperative orientation. Similarly, God engineers natural consequences into our experiences with life, so that we come to know his thinking behind the order of creation. He has always concerned himself with developing in us a cooperative *relationship* with him.

Now consider a somewhat different view of Christ's sacrifice from that which we usually hear. Christ died not so much to benefit persons, as to benefit the *relationship* between those persons and God. In 1 Peter 3:18, we read that he died that he might bring us to God. Like a matchmaker, Christ weds us to our Maker. Not just coincidentally, this verse comes right after instructions to husbands concerning their marital responsibilities.

Christ did not die so that we could live *instead* of him, but so that we could live *with* him. The former, mistaken idea sounds as if Christ said, "There's only room for one of us in the lifeboat, so I'll let you live while I drown." Neither partner in a vital relationship becomes a nobody so that the other can be a somebody. Both invest their somebodyness in a radiant relationship.

"Worthwhile" Implies "To Someone"

To say a person has worth or value formulates only half a sentence. It begs two questions and raises a third: *Worth what? To whom? Who says?* These questions reveal a search for a source, a valuer, an authority behind the action of attaching worth. This quest implies our awareness of a person larger than us, who initiates relationships with us.

Our parents stood as the original superhumans in whose eyes we wanted much worth. Now as adults, when we feel worth*less*, we ache with the dangling half-question, *Do I have any value?* We used to seek evidence from Mom and Dad of our importance to them. Though we no longer look to them as our source, we have not yet identified a new one. We spin our wheels with the unanswered questions of our half-sentences. We wistfully yearn for some authority to come along and fill those gaps that our parents left.

The Christian message emphatically completes the half-sentence. What are we worth? To whom? "God so greatly loved and dearly prized the world that He [even] gave up His only begotten Son, so that whoever believes in (trusts, clings to, relies on) Him may not perish — come to destruction, be lost — but have eternal (everlasting) life" (John 3:16 AMPLIFIED).

As reassuring as the above words sound they do not always quench our desperate thirst for a sense of personal significance. Why? Maybe because we have two electromagnets near us, each capable of attracting and holding us. Jesus alluded to them in this penetrating admonition to the most stubborn, strong-willed adults he faced, the scribes and Pharisees: "So for the sake of your tradition (the rules handed down by your forefathers), you have set aside the Word of God — depriving it of force and authority and making it of no effect" (Matt. 15:6 AMPLIFIED).

It's as if Jesus is telling us that we have two switches at our fingertips. One sends current to the Word-of-God magnet, the other to the human-heritage magnet. By our will, we choose which magnet to empower. When we do not find comfort in the words of God's love in John 3:16, it's a sure sign that we are somehow choosing to switch energy into the nonsense we began believing early in life as mistaken participants in a world of deluded thinkers.

Near the end of his life, the same apostle John wrote a letter. An old man with great wisdom, he cautioned his readers: "Little children, keep yourselves from idols — false gods, [from anything and everything that would occupy the place in your heart due to God, from any sort of substitute for Him that would take first place in your life]. . ." (1 John 5:21 AMPLIFIED).

We qualify as little children. And we need to root ourselves in the only valid authority, the God whom John heard Jesus call "Father." Therefore, to cure our own emptiness, we must magnify his fullness. The more we deliberately value his greatness, the more we feel the compliment of his valuing us.

Self-worth comes as a by-product of worshiping God.

6

Mind Renewing

Jewish people from every country — Mesopotamia, Judea, Rome, Libya and Egypt — filled the streets of Jerusalem. They had crowded there to celebrate Pentecost, the Feast of Weeks.

Simon Peter stood and addressed the crowd. He explained the death and resurrection of Jesus, and the people responded to his sermon brokenheartedly. They pleaded with Peter to tell them what they should do to change the sinful condition he had exposed in them.

He told them to repent, to change their views. He also told them to be baptized, to take a specific action consistent with their new views (Acts 2:38). This passage reveals two realities.

First, we hold our views and intentions directly under our own power and ability to choose. We construct our own attitudes and motivations. Otherwise, the command, "Repent!" would be impossible, absurd, and unfair.

Second, the new attitudes and actions we deliberately

choose should reflect the authority that Christ already has over us. That explains the act of baptism "in Jesus' name."

How, then, do we change our minds and our behavior? Paul showed us one way to handle the dilemma when he said, "Do not conform any longer to the pattern of this world, but be transformed by the renewing of your mind. Then you will be able to test and approve what God's will is — his good, pleasing and perfect will" (Rom. 12:2).

Labeling with Purpose

Romans 12:2 teaches that we change our living by changing our thinking. The simplest changes we can make involve the labels we attach to events in our lives. We can use our negative feelings as windows into our souls. We can look in, or listen in, and detect what names we call things, that make us feel toward them as we do. Then we can consider what other labels could apply. We can dramatically change our feelings toward a person, thing, or event by selecting a positive label from the list.

What do you see right now? A book? Paper and ink? Black and white? English words? Written language? Sentences and paragraphs? A commercial product? An author's thoughts?

Which of these terms correctly identifies the one, single, right label to attach to what you see in front of you? Of course! No single one alone gives *the* true label — all are correct. The name you select to represent what you see depends on what purpose you have in mind.

The same principle applies to the circumstances we face in life. We can call each one by several valid names. We choose labels that help us to accomplish our goals. The labels we choose determine how we feel and what we do.

A perfectionistic student who insists on getting straight

A's on every school assignment might think of a B on an exam as "cruel and unusual punishment." His predictable mood might include: irritation, depression, brooding, thoughts of telling off the teacher, ideas of quitting school altogether. He might savagely increase his determination to stay up later, study harder, and never again allow such an unthinkable disaster to occur.

That student could create much more manageable feelings by regarding the B grade as "a mild disappointment, an inconvenience, a tolerably unpleasant outcome," or even as "above-average performance."

I protect my marriage from the ravages of my strong-willed tendencies by persisting in positively relabeling my wife's words, actions, and intentions. I'm supersensitive to having a fault pointed out in me. One day my wife, Ruth, told me that I had dominated a conversation we held with a friend, and that I had not given our friend a chance to speak her mind.

At first impulse I wanted to defend myself, but I deliberately held back and quickly prayed in silence, "Thank you, God, for allowing Ruth to mention this to me. Is there something here you want me to learn?" After a second or two, I realized that I agreed with her. I took a giant step forward for me and deliberately said, "I think you're right."

In my mind I had done all that anyone could reasonably expect of me at that point. I had gone the second, third, and fourth miles with Ruth, and expected her to say, "Okay," and drop the subject. Instead, she continued, "Yes, I think I am right because Martha needed a chance to talk. She was all bottled up with feelings, and you didn't give her a chance to express them."

That statement from Ruth, even though she said it calmly and kindly, caused me pain. I felt humiliated and burned, telling myself that Ruth *wanted* to roast me for a crime already confessed and forgiven.

Ruth and I had discussed this pattern between us and my effort to change my part in it. Therefore, this time I did not retaliate with anger as I had done in the past, always to Ruth's bewilderment. I realized that she did not *intend* to singe me after I said that I agreed with her. In fact, her continuing to talk had almost nothing to do with me. She merely wanted to further clarify her own thoughts on the incident by expressing them aloud to me. I relabeled her action from "roasting me" to "thinking out loud." Then I felt better toward her.

By error, I tend to assume that Ruth expects some further response from me. I *imagine* that she wants me to crawl on my hands and knees, confess that I am wicked and terrible, and vow I'll never do it again. She doesn't want that. She just wants to put *her* thoughts together. If anything, she wants from me only permission to assemble her thoughts, say them, and find relief. Maybe at most she would like a grunt from me, or perhaps, "I'm with you, honey."

Like conversions to Christ, sometimes our mind renewals occur instantaneously, similar to medical student Gary's change from "because" to "even though." Other times it happens gradually, like a child growing up in a Christian home, or like my deliberate, year-after-year changing of my perception of Ruth's intentions, when she continues to talk about my misdeeds after I have agreed to regard them as misdeeds.

Positive Relabeling

We can learn to recognize the positive intention behind what other people say and do as a key to positive relabeling. One husband reacted furiously to his wife's frequent comments, grimaces, and groans about his driving. He regarded her actions as "criticism." Using that label, he made *himself* mad at her, as he worked himself into feeling small and resentful. He searched for another label for her actions and came up with "request." He recognized that, besides criticizing him, his wife was also requesting that he slow down, allow more space behind the car ahead, and come to stops more gradually. These he easily did, to his wife's great relief and appreciation. Thinking of himself as "granting my wife's requests" gave him a feeling of masculine magnanimity.

Strong-willed adults generally cling to the notion that criticism directed at them poses an unthinkably dreadful assault, one for them to ward off and neutralize by severe counterattacks against the critic. But in John 18:23 Jesus vividly shows us a realistic adult's attitude toward criticism.

Having just received verbal and physical slaps for not answering the high priest's illegal question, Jesus responded with the following attitudes: (a) If I am wrong, I want to know it; please point out the godly principle I violated; (b) if I am not evil or mistaken in what I said, I am curious about your motivation in punishing me. I ask you to consider what motivates you: what goals, purposes, and standards are you pursuing? What authority do you obey? Who or what is your god?

We can adopt similar attitudes toward criticism. We can challenge our old notion that it lowers our self-esteem, and then take it as information about ourselves from which we can benefit. We can also take information about others for a loving confrontation with them for their benefit.

I find that I can employ the same approach with self-criticism. I fall short of my godly ambitions every time I look through my old nature's goggles of gloom. But with the eyes of my new nature I call these shortcomings something altogether different. I no longer consider them *failures*, but *opportunities to learn.* I stop regarding inferiority feelings as crushing curses, and welcome them as valuable information on places I have yet to grow. They let me know what muscles Coach God seeks to develop in me, so that I can increase in usefulness to him.

Creative Imaging

A young man — we'll call him Jim — worked in public relations with a nonprofit agency. He overly concerned himself with gaining approval. When he sensed people might react unfavorably toward him, he could hardly think of anything else. His inordinate need for commendation interfered with his efficiency at work.

Then he began to use his imagination in connection with Paul's words to young Timothy: "Do your best to present yourself to God as one approved, a workman who does not need to be ashamed and who correctly handles the word of truth" (2 Tim. 2:15).

Jim developed a whole new meaning to the word *approved.* He visualized himself as an unashamed workman standing before God. He saw God hand him a sword (the Word of Truth), and commission him to go forth in radiant Government Issue uniform (the mark of approval in God's kingdom), swinging that sword as necessary in the King's service.

Approved now meant for him "selected and sent" by God, at *God's* initiative, not Jim's! He wept with relief from the burden of having to earn acceptance again and again. He experienced more fully, in his inward being, the meaning of that familiar Scripture that says salvation is "... the gift of God — not by works, so that no one can boast" (Eph. 2:8, 9).

Getting Our Head Together

Recent neuropsychological research on the brain suggests that its two halves specialize in complementary functions. One side controls the process of logic, reasoning, calculating, using language — what we experience as conscious and voluntary. The other side controls our more nearly unconscious functions of visualizing, dreaming, feeling, making stories, producing artistic creations.

In most of our efforts to change, we hammer away with the verbal, logical side, trying to talk ourselves into behaving as we should. We can greatly aid that process by adding to our logical audio some brilliant video from the other side of the brain. In so doing, we literally get our head together. We can create experiences in our imagination that have as powerful an effect upon our subsequent attitudes and emotions as any past experiences that have happened to us. Ruth Carter Stapleton, in *The Gift of Inner Healing* (1976), referred to this technique of inner-child healing as "faith-imagination."

We can modify the word *imagination* slightly to make it "image-in-action" — mental movies. Note how near we come to the heart of God with our creative visualizing. Since he created us in his image, when we create images in our minds, we imitate him. This supremely characterizes beloved children! They constantly try to do things like their fathers do.

I once enhanced my experience of solidarity with a small prayer group by making a mental movie. As we sat enjoying a silent prayer time together, I pictured each of us as a photoelectric cell that responds to sunlight by generating electric power. The Son of God became the Sun of God in my mind, beaming upon each of us in that group. In praying, each of us injected power into the whole body that we comprised.

Electric companies place generating stations at strategic points in an interlocking network of power lines. If a breakdown occurs in any part of that grid, power can shift from a different section of the country to make up the lack. This gives us a modern-day parable of the body of Christ. We generate when we pray for others or speak words of encouragement to them. We put energy into that network to which we belong. At other times, when we hurt, we can draw encouragement from the group, just as a consumer draws electric power from the grid by turning on the lights at home.

By deliberately creating mental movies of myself giving electrical power into the grid, and drawing some out, I increase my sense of connectedness to the body of Christ. I am neither a reject nor a superior, but an active participant among equals.

Sometimes creating godly pictures in our minds can help us to improve painful relationships.

Seeing Is Believing

A devout Christian young man lamented that he just couldn't let go of bitterness he felt about certain mental wounds he had suffered years earlier. He could quote Scriptures about how he should forgive, but he still didn't *feel* forgiving. He had prayed repeatedly, "Thank you, God, for letting such-and-such happen in my life." Still, he didn't *feel* thankful.

Then he used the idea that one picture is worth a thousand words. He pictured the wrongs done to him as gashes cutting deeply into his body. Then he imagined himself as a giant key, and those gashes took on new meaning. They became notches precisely machined along the edge of the key to make it uniquely useful. God could use him as a tool to fit locks that no other key could budge.

The locks represented bitterness, fear, and discouragement in the minds of other people. Now he, the notched key, could understand them. The hurts in his life had made him useful to other people's lives. He wept and laughed as he visualized God's huge hands turning him, the key, in those locks and freeing others from their emotional prisons.

Another time I met a sincere Christian woman who knew many passages of Scripture, and often had deep, personal experiences of worship and closeness to God. Yet she repeatedly fell into the old habit of criticizing her family members. When they made noise, or didn't do what she wanted them to do, she would lash out in a biting, sarcastic, hurtful way toward her husband and her children. Then she would say again and again, "God, please forgive me. I know I shouldn't do that. I try, but I can't help myself. I want to hold my tongue, but I also want to give in to the temptation and blow up just like my mother used to do."

Her breakthrough came in a psychotherapy session in which she visualized herself as a little child again, watching her mother and father argue. She imagined their mouths and tongues multiplying and falling out on the ground, going two-forty, biting, and chattering. They looked like the wind-up teeth sold in novelty stores. She saw millions of these lying around on the ground, and noticed that she, as a child, had picked one up and stuffed it into her own mouth. She used this *borrowed* mouth and tongue anytime she criticized her family. It didn't belong to her in the first place. She had borrowed it from Mom and Dad.

Next, as a grown woman, she visualized Jesus entering the picture. He stood by her to take care of that mouth and tongue. As he stood there with his hands open, she took out that old mouth and tongue and put them into his hands. He took them like a lump of clay, squeezed them in his powerful hands, and molded them into something new.

Then she thought of the Scripture where Isaiah said, ". . . I am a man of unclean lips, and I live among a people of unclean lips" (6:5). What did Isaiah do in his faith-imagination? He saw a seraph, an angelic creature, take a hot coal from a burning altar and put it on Isaiah's lips to purify them.

The woman loved that Scripture and applied it to herself. She saw a hot coal disinfect the hole in her face, and then Jesus put in a new mouth and a new tongue. Instead of criticism, the new mouth and tongue spoke words of sweetness and praise. The woman connected this mental movie with specific Scriptures that she knew and loved. The next week she reported to me, "You wouldn't believe how different my husband is this week!"

Sometimes, though, all the imagination in the world will not correct a situation. Fractured relationships can receive full healing only by asking and granting forgiveness.

7

Stepping-Stones
to Forgiveness

Let your imagination picture a special Sunday morning. You have just entered a uniquely honest worship service at The First Church of the Strong-Willed. The congregation sings lustily their first hymn: "My hope is built on nothing less than my old hurts and bitterness."

Clinging to Unforgiveness

Strong-willed adults often cling to unforgiveness as if it offered life itself. They fear they'll die if they let go of their bitterness. In one sense they are absolutely correct! They *will* die — to the security that keeps them shrouded in a hard, unyielding shell.

People often say in counseling that they think they have committed the unpardonable sin. Upon questioning, though, they usually reveal an unwillingness to pardon God or someone else. While it may not ultimately condemn them to eternity separated from God, an unwillingness to participate in the process of forgiveness toward others blocks the personal forgiveness they could receive so freely from him now.

Jesus offered a short commentary after he gave the Lord's Prayer. He could have expanded on any number of the exquisitely concise statements in his model conversation with God. But he chose the part about forgiving debts. He said, "Amen," to the prayer, and then added that if we don't forgive our debtors, our heavenly Father won't forgive us our debts to him.

I used to have trouble with that apparent tit-for-tat approach on God's part. He seemed kind of small, like a kid on a playground saying, "You make the first move, and then I'll do my part." That concept didn't fit the great God who split the Red Sea. Then I realized that God never holds back from forgiving me, but literally, in the nature of things, he *cannot* forgive me until I have forgiven someone else.

God opens his arms wide to embrace me — and for me to embrace him — in a hug of reconciliation and forgiveness. I cannot open my arms to join in that hug as long as I clutch in them a list of grievances, a stack of IOUs, a ledger of accounts receivable from my debtors. I have a choice to make: either hang on and cherish those grudges, those hurts, those resentments from the past, or drop them and join the embrace with God. He waits. He says, "As long as you hold on to those, there's no way you and I can get together. It's up to you. I'm willing." But God cannot force his forgiveness on someone who does not choose forgiveness.

When we refuse to forgive, the strong-willed child within us clings to childish attitudes and resentments. Yet the apostle Paul tells us, "When I was a child, I talked like a child, I thought like a child, I reasoned like a child. When I became a man, I put childish ways behind me" (1 Cor. 13:11).

Many people never leave childish ways behind them, because they refuse with a vengeance to do their mothers and fathers the honor of forgiving them. Satan has a heyday with people who keep themselves stuck in childhood by resenting Mom and Dad. He steers them away from saying, "Well, Mom and Dad did the best they could. They gave me what they knew how to give me, and I love them. I accept them the way they were. In fact, I specifically appreciate the way they taught me _____."

Those words stick right below the Adam's apple for persons who feel a lot of bitterness. Why? Because Satan keeps his propaganda before them, saying, "Look out. If you dare appreciate your parents, you will come under their cruel power. They will crush you beneath their merciless heels." Cartoonist Gary Larson's "vegetables" cartoon shows the kind of cruel power that some people seem to think their parents have.

Satan spreads lies. We stay in the prison of immaturity by believing the delusion that if we rebel and resent our parents hard enough and long enough, we can declare our own power. When we continue to fight skirmishes in a war long since finished, we actually forsake our freedom to live life.

Finding the Way of Life

The way of life requires us to accept our parents for who they were and what they did for us, and to forgive them for who they were not and what they did not do for us. Modern medicine and psychology have discovered that resentment affects the tissues of our bodies and shortens our lives. When we honor Father and Mother, we let go of resentment.

**"Why, yes . . . we do have two children who won't eat
their vegetables."**

We forgive them and become free; our physical bodies become free from the continual drip of acid inside of us.

Yet the act of forgiveness often involves a process that
seldom happens easily. Psychotherapists make their living
helping people struggle through the process, which evolves
a lot like mourning. Both forgiveness and grief ask us to let

go of something old in order to appropriate something new. Like any difficult task, we can handle forgiveness more easily if we take one step at a time. The following five stepping stones to forgiveness all begin with the letter A.

Step One: *Acknowledge* the Loss

Roger always wanted a dad who would sit down with him and teach him how to use tools. In his fantasy, Dad would say, "Son, here's how you do this, here's how you do that. Thatta boy. You're getting it. Try it again. You can do it. A little more to the left. Now a little more to the right. You *did* it! Nice job! I'm proud of you!"

Roger dreamed his fantasy often, but it didn't come true. He acknowledges now that it didn't, and that his heart still yearns for it. He has taken the first step in grieving, by acknowledging his loss.

In order to move from grief to forgiveness, I must acknowledge that my offender broke *God's* law in hurting me. If I had had a father like Roger's, I must agree that Dad violated God's assignment of the father role to him, by not spending time with me. This becomes an important test for me. If Dad merely failed to satisfy my preferences, but did not violate God's laws, I have no case. When the offender really did wrong in God's eyes, I must agree with God, and not whitewash my grievances.

I can help increase the therapeutic impact of acknowledging the wrong done to me by adding a mental movie to my thoughts. I picture a courtroom in heaven. An archangel has just described my offender's sin against me. The evidence speaks for itself. God, Moses, and a million angels raise their hands in a vote of "Guilty!" against my offender. I see myself raising my hand along with them all, agreeing with God's verdict in the matter. I join God as an ally rather than pursue a private vendetta of my own.

Step Two: *Admit* Tender Feelings

The second step in the grief and forgiveness process asks me to *admit my own tender feelings*, to go beyond my resentment, hurt, and anger. Those surface emotions cover deeper feelings of sadness and love.

Perhaps a woman remembers, "When Dad was mean to me my heart broke. Sadness overwhelmed me. I so much wanted his love and understanding, and he didn't show them to me time after time that he hit me."

Perhaps a man like Roger admits how much he admired the dad who disappointed him. He recalls Dad's manliness, his tool chest, his ability with his hands. He remembers a marvelous man who could fix anything. How much he really loved his dad with a child's awe!

Love always lurks beneath bitterness; otherwise our resentments would lack energy. We can resent only what we once treasured.

To go further in Step Two, I admit that my hurt did not so much sting as it left me with a deep sense of loss. In the heavenly courtroom of my mental movie, in front of the same heavenly jury, I imagine myself reaching into my wallet and pulling forth an old photograph of the loved one who hurt me long ago. I see myself revealing to the surrounding witnesses that I secretly cherished that memento all these years.

Step Three: *Absorbing* the Loss

One version of the Lord's Prayer says, "Forgive us our *debts* as we forgive our debtors." Everyone innately understands the law of indebtedness: when a man wrongs me, he becomes my debtor; he unbalances a sort of equity between us that requires restoration. When I act vengefully, I insist on settling that account by inflicting a compensatory injury upon my offender.

But when I forgive and absorb a loss, like that of a cruelty from my father, I say, "All right, Dad did me wrong, but I no longer require repayment from him. I hereby absorb the loss of his love, and the pain of his wrong to me. Yes, I felt great hurt, but I stop the buck here."

Jesus did that for us at the cross. He personally absorbed the cruelty of our wrongs against God, the loneliness of our breaches of relationship with him. By his own choice, God loves us and does not want alienation from us. He says, "Rather than just whip them to get even with them, I will absorb the loss. It costs me to have them break off their relationships with me, and I willingly pay that price myself." That explains the meaning of Christ's death. When we were bankrupt, Jesus paid the debt of our enormous damages toward God. He said, "I will absorb the loss in my own body and not require it of them."

So I say of Dad when I absorb the loss, "I no longer demand any restitution from him. I wipe the slate clean. I set his balance now at zero. He owes me nothing for what he has done." I choose never again to use my loss as a kind of IOU from Dad to me. I pursue no further bargaining, such as, "Because you didn't give me such-and-such when I was a kid, at least you owe me a loan to help me buy this car that I want now. In view of all the wrongs you did against me then, you *have* to do something good for me today."

No! I *cancel* his debt to me. If he owed me the equivalent of ten thousand dollars, I say to him, "As of today you no longer owe me a single dollar. I am going to bear that cost." I have no claim, no leverage with which to recover damages. I stand empty-handed, finally free to receive from God better than what I craved in my greedy, clinging bitterness.

As a visual aid to my decision to absorb the loss, I imagine Jesus walking toward me out of that crowd of courtroom witnesses. He comes as the expert on absorbing losses. He now entrusts me, as his faithful disciple, with some similar work to do.

He hands me a sponge. Then he points to a puddle of spilled milk that symbolizes the wrong done against me. I step forward, kneel, and soak that sponge thoroughly with the spilled milk. I walk over to a convenient porthole that leads to the Lake of Fire. I wring the sponge dry into that porthole, incinerating the spilled milk of Dad's wrongdoing to me. Three times I sponge and wring. The third time, the puddle disappears; not a trace remains . . . *anywhere.* As an agent of Christ, I have shown the whole assembly that my offender owes me nothing and has no mess to clean up in my soul.

Step Four: *Abandon* the Use of My Memories as Weapons

People often say, "I can forgive, but I just can't forget." Of course we cannot forget. God has so made us that everything we ever experience remains indelibly recorded in biochemical tissue in our brains. God gave us memory as a gift. Therefore, we choose what use we will make of our memory, whether to harm or heal.

Before forgiving, I use a particular memory as a weapon, or as a means of leverage against my offender. In forgiving, I still hold the memory of the wrong done to me. Then, to abandon the use of it as a weapon, I decide I will never again, even in the heat of an argument, mention the wrong in such a way as to punish, embarrass, manipulate, or obligate my offender. I remove that option from my own tool kit as if I never had it.

It helps to picture a particular memory I cannot seem to

forget, in the form of an arrow in the quiver of my mind. I lift it out, take it in my two hands, break it, and drop it into the nearby Lake of Fire that consumes it forever.

Step Five: *Appreciate*

Having ruled out destructive directions for my memories, I still have them available for some kind of use. They will not long remain unassigned, but will soon return to guerrilla warfare in my subconscious mind *if* I do not consciously reassign them to peacetime constructive efforts. I can salvage valuable nuggets from painful experiences.

Appreciation provides the antidote for the poison of bitterness. To appreciate that which I do not like requires my fundamental reexamination of God's part in my ordeal. It requires me to reconsider what I really believe about his character.

I reason like this: God knew what I was going through. He could have spared me from the hardship that I underwent, but he didn't. He allowed me to experience the mom who hit me, or the dad who didn't teach me how to use tools, or the older brother who did not encourage my manhood. God allowed all that pain for a purpose consistent with his good and loving nature and his determination to fashion me into something resembling himself. Therefore, I thank him for the experience, even before I *feel* thankful, even before I know *how* the experience benefited me. While *only* God knows what it did for me, I agree that he, like any other good father, often holds secrets in his marvelous mind.

By giving thanks I take a step of faith and obedience. I do not act hypocritically when I *give* thanks without *feeling* thankful. Hypocrisy means that I claim to follow a certain authority, then don't. God commands his children to give thanks. I pledge my allegiance to God, not to my feelings, as my guide.

Therefore, I go ahead and *try* to find something to value about my hurtful experience. And what do I hear in my head? "This one doesn't count. This tragedy registered higher on the Richter scale than any that a person should ever have to endure. I am sure nobody could find anything to appreciate about the horrible hardship and uncommon abuse that I have suffered in this instance."

Then I deliberately reflect, "Okay, God, thank you for that situation, for that particular episode I am remembering when Dad hit me. That really hurt. But thank you for what you taught me in that situation. Because, now that I think of it, I behaved kind of irresponsibly around that age. Thank you that Dad cared enough to do *something* to let me know that he found my behavior unacceptable.

"Also, thank you for the times when Dad treated me wrongly and unfairly, and punished me unjustly. Thank you for giving me a little bit of an experience that helps me understand what your Son went through during his trial and murder for a crime that he did not commit. I thank you that you gave me a chance long ago as a kid to record a memory that now enables me to understand your heart and your program a little better. You really did something for me! I worship you in a whole new way. I feel better and more insightful than I ever did before. I appreciate that painful thing that happened to me long ago."

When applying appreciation to my grief, I appreciate that while I mourn a loss, "loss" means I had something for a while. I remember little snatches of what I *did* have. Then, like Roger mentioned earlier, I muse, "God, thank you for the times that Dad showed me how to use a screwdriver. I sure wish he also would have shown me how to use the electric drill, the hammer, and those fourteen different kinds of saws that he had. Anyway, I do remember the time he taught me how to use a screwdriver, and showed me the difference between a Phillips head and a regular head. I always think of that every time I use a Phillips screwdriver."

Hitting a Roadblock

These steps to forgiveness offer no cure-all. You may try them and somewhere along the line hit a roadblock. You go ahead and mechanically say the words, but something inside of you says, No, I am not going to admit that I really love Dad; I just can't bring myself to say that. What then?

Welcome it as a great opportunity to learn a little bit more about yourself. When you come to a block like that, deliberately exaggerate your resistance, your reluctance. Go even further with it. Feed it. Say things like, "I will not. Never in a thousand years. I don't care how God bakes me in hell, or whatever he does to me. I'll never, never, never admit that I love my father, because if I did, it would be as if I were really reaching out and touching Dad, and that I vow in my deepest soul to strictly refuse forevermore. World without end. Amen."

A picture of what you hunger for — what you wanted that you have not yet let yourself know — may come into focus. If you exaggerate your oyster of resentment, you can discover the pearl it hides. Recognize your pain and resentment as symptoms of the love and desire you once felt. Admit it to yourself first, then to God, and then to the person. If your parents have died, you can still do this in a psychodrama. Put an empty chair in front of you and imagine your father there, and tell him you love him. Talk it back and forth. It helps if you do that with someone else, especially with a trained person who can foster the dialogue and help you finish your grieving.

As a psychotherapist I repeatedly see in operation the natural law of family influences dramatically phrased by

God to Israel in giving the second commandment: ". . . I, the LORD your God, am a jealous God, punishing the children for the sin of the fathers to the third and fourth generation of those who hate me, but showing love to thousands who love me and keep my commandments" (Deut. 5:9,10). I picture this curse of the generations as a chain made of links — grandparents, parents, children. Three generations shackled to each other by reciprocal wrongdoing and resentment rooted in disregard for God's majesty and authority.

That's the bad news. Now the good news: you can break that curse at your link in the chain! You can go to the second side of the "but" in that Deuteronomy passage, and institute a new heritage based on love and obedience toward God. The fifth A of forgiveness does precisely that.

Years ago country singers recorded a song called, "I'm My Own Grandpa." As long as I nurse resentment and bitterness toward my father, I maintain an unholy sibling rivalry with his immature side. When instead I express heartfelt appreciation to my father, I fulfill the role that Grandfather *should* have exercised, that of blessing my father.

Thus, I break myself out of the chain by going back a link and feeding the link ahead of me. I honor my father and my mother by not insisting that they give me what I wanted, but by giving to them the manna of acceptance for which everyone hungers. What I wanted *from* them I give *to* them. I thus find *my* freedom and discover the deep wisdom that Jesus knew: "It is more blessed to give than to receive."

Saying Eulogies Now

Say your eulogies to your loved ones while they can still hear them. If your parents are living, go to them and tell them the precious memories you have. This becomes an important way of forgiving them, of saying good-bye to them now, so that at the time of their funeral, you won't need to say, "If only I would have told them so-and-so." Tell them *now*!

Some years ago I went to my mom and dad together, and told them all the precious, specific memories that I have about them. I told Dad a particularly special one: "Dad, I remember one time when I must have been about three or four years old. It was a Sunday, because you were sitting there reading the big newspaper you had in your lap. I was across the room from you, pushing the vacuum cleaner back and forth, with the cord all wound up, not plugged in. I was pretending to vacuum, playing house, helping Mom.

"I remember as clear as a bell, Dad, that you laid down your paper, looked at me with strength and love in your face, and said, 'Den, why don't you plug the cord in and really vacuum?' I want you to know how proud I was, that my dad thought I was grown up enough to help Mom really vacuum."

When I told him that, his eyes filled. He said he didn't remember the time, but he was glad that I told him. Months later at a Thanksgiving family gathering, Dad asked me, "Den, do you remember the time you pretended to vacuum, and I told you to plug it in?" He had recorded it as his own memory. We can call into being lovely things that were not there before our speaking.

Forgiving God

In addition to forgiving others, we all face a key decision: whether or not we will forgive God. We could file a damage suit against him in the Universal Court of Appeals. There we can press for vindication, for a verdict against God, finding him guilty of gross negligence in the line of duty, since he so blatantly blundered in inflicting our parents upon us.

We have one alternative: accept God's plan for our lives. A mental movie might help us. We can picture ourselves with God in heaven before our birth. We see the whole story lying ahead of us, and then consent for him to deliver us as vulnerable infants into the care of such faulty parents as our moms and dads.

We shed some of the shackles of unforgiveness when we actually say words like these: "God, I agree to become a small girl, in the home of a hard father who tells me he would rather have had a son. I am willing to have an anxious mother overprotect me and thus deprive me of the chance to learn grown-up skills at an early age. In short, I consent to have you entrust my well-being to amateurs.

"God of Abraham, Isaac, and Jacob, Mom and Dad, and me, what a fantastic program you have under way. What liberty you give me, even to thumb my nose at you, to say *no* to your outreaching arms. I really crack when I run that kind of risk with people, and they say *no* to me. It gives me great security to know that you are not fragile; you don't take insult, but you find new, creative ways to come around and caress me, and invite me to you.

"Thank you for your creativity in the cross, where your Son, Jesus, in whose name I address you, said, 'Father, forgive them. They just don't realize what they're doing.' "

Reconciling with the Forgiven

Paula suffered physical abuse from two men in her life, her father and her husband. She forgave both, but reconciled only with her father, because only he made it possible.

Forgiveness I perform between God and me about another person's wrong against me. *Reconciliation* I bring about between the person who has wronged me and me — a person whom I have forgiven, *and who has resolved not to wrong me again in that way.* Forgiving does not mean foolishly returning to an abusive situation, like Sylvia's unwise passenger advises her in the "Anywhere" cartoon by Gary Larson.

Forgiving means removing my bitterness as an obstacle to reconciliation. It means my willingness to rebuild with

"C'mon, Sylvia . . . where's your spirit of adventure?"

a willing partner who shares with me a commitment to a nonabusive partnership in the future. It also means my *un*willingness to reinstitute a past way of relating with a partner not committed to build with me a new way of relating that guards against repeats of an abusive past.

Paula forgave her father in her heart with a counselor's assistance. She had not spoken with him for years. Now as a married adult, she called him, told him her love, said she wanted to be friends, and arranged a get-together for lunch. It moved him deeply, and he readily agreed to their lunch date.

As they talked over lunch, Dad kept the conversation light, mostly catching up on news from the missing years, and wishing Paula well. She would have liked from him a confession and apology for his physical abuse toward her years before; but he remained a proud and fearful man who would not humble himself to offer such a confession directly. He indirectly did his part toward reconciling simply by abundantly expressing goodwill.

Paula did not insist that Dad take responsibility for his past actions toward her because she and Dad were not laying groundwork to return to the kind of relationship they once had. Paula and her father never again would find themselves in a situation where he could abuse her as a child dependent upon his provision and protection. Paula's inward forgiveness of her father, coupled with his outward friendliness, provided sufficient ingredients for their reconciliation.

Paula also forgave her husband, Peter, inwardly, and he expressed outward friendliness to her, but they could not reconcile because Peter would not confess and repent of his past physical abuse toward her. Peter said that he was sorry if he had hurt Paula, but that she should not frustrate him to the point where he blows up. He proposed that they put the past behind them. He said that he loved her. He played on her guilt feelings by implying that she should not call herself a Christian if she would not forgive him by canceling her legal restraining order and letting him back into the house. In none of these manipulations did Peter take responsibility for having hurt Paula, nor did he express any awareness of wrongdoing on his part, nor did he indicate any openness to hearing from Paula what she considered wrong about what he did.

For Paula and Peter, to reconcile meant to rebuild a damaged covenantal relationship in which each one's well-being depended on the partner's trustworthiness. Peter had broken the trust and the covenant repeatedly in the past by his abusive actions. To build anew with Paula, Peter had to agree with her on the wrong he had done, and on a plan to protect their relationship from similar injury in the future. This plan had to give power to the former victim, Paula, to protect herself against any future attacks from Peter that seemed imminent to her.

Peter would not accompany Paula to a counselor, protesting that nobody else needed to know about their problems, and that they, as two intelligent persons, could solve their own, which weren't very big after all. Paula wisely went to a counselor alone anyway and learned how to love tough. She told Peter that she wanted to reconcile with him and that she would under certain conditions: (1) he would admit that he had done wrong by abusing her; (2) he would pledge not to abuse her again in the future; (3) he would work out with her a mutually acceptable plan whereby she could take immediate unilateral action to protect herself if she feared that he might soon abuse her; (4) the two of them would work out these three matters with a counselor's help, to the satisfaction of each, before they would resume living together.

Peter never agreed to these conditions. He repeatedly tried to get Paula to set aside these responsible requirements regulating respect. Like a typical strong-willed adult, Peter said things like, "If you really loved me you'd *want* me back in the house. Why do you need rules; don't you trust me? Are you calling me a liar? You have some pretty bad psychological problems if you can't even bring yourself to trust the people who love you." Paula, with the counselor's encouragement, held firm that she *would* let Peter back in, only under the above conditions. Peter angrily said that he could see when he wasn't wanted, and that Paula was not the only fish in the ocean. A couple months later Paula heard that Peter had begun living with a woman, whom he also abused.

Accountability

Forgiving we do inside ourselves, between God and ourselves. Reconciling we do between ourselves and a person who has wronged us, whom we have forgiven. When in reconciling I say, "I forgive you," I mean that I agree with my offender about the seriousness of the offense, and the adequacy of our preparations to prevent its recurrence. I also make myself *accountable* (there's a sixth A) to the person I forgive as one way to make forgiveness a permanent transaction. I can bind myself to my offender, for example, by saying, "I promise never again to mention this matter in such a way as to hurt you. If it ever seems to you that I bring it up to use it against you, will you please tell me so, and remind me of this promise?"

Accountability like this shows us the other side of a coin. The bitterness we feel in response to wrongs done to us calls for us to *ask* as well as to grant forgiveness. We ask forgiveness by the deliberate, thorough process of confession and repentance.

8

Contentment Through Repentance

Strong-willed adult:	Please forgive me.
God:	*For what wrong?*
Strong-willed adult:	Oh, I lost my temper at the kids.
God:	*So what?*
Strong-willed adult:	What do you mean?
God:	*What wrong did you commit when you lost your temper at the kids?*
Strong-willed adult:	Well, you don't want me to, do you?
God:	*You haven't answered the question I asked you.*
Strong-willed adult:	What did you ask me?
God:	*What wrong did you commit when you lost your temper at the kids?*
Strong-willed adult:	You're telling me now that I didn't commit a wrong?

God: I *didn't say that. I am asking you what* **you** *think you did wrong when you lost your temper at the kids.*

Strong-willed adult: Look, I'm sorry! All right? What more does a guy have to do, bleed or something?

God: *No, Jesus my Son has already taken care of that.*

Strong-willed adult: Well, what am I supposed to do?

God: *To accomplish what?*

Strong-willed adult: To be forgiven for blowing up at the kids.

God: *Tell me what you think you did wrong when you blew up at the kids.*

Strong-willed adult: All right, I did wrong because I shouldn't blow up!

God: *Why not?*

Strong-willed adult: You really confuse me. Here I am, apologizing because I broke one of your rules, and you give me a hard time over it.

God: *Do you know what is really happening between us?*

Strong-willed adult: No, what?

God: *I have asked you a central question that relates to your request of me. And you, instead of doing the hard work of thinking about the question seriously, accuse me of mistreating you.*

Strong-willed adult: I'm sorry.

God: *For what wrong?*

Strong-willed adult: Oh, no, here we go again. Can't you just say, "Okay, I forgive you for accusing me"?

God:	*Forgiveness involves a meeting of two minds concerning the nature of some wrong done. So far, you have not made clear to me what you think you did wrong when you lost your temper at the kids.*
Strong-willed adult:	Well, *you* think I did wrong, don't you?
God:	*You tried that one on me already.*
Strong-willed adult:	What do you mean?
God:	*You already tried to toss the ball to me and get me to bawl you out, instead of answering the question of what you think you did wrong when you blew your top at the kids.*
Strong-willed adult:	Okay, I give up. What do you want from me?
God:	*This conversation started because you wanted something from me, remember? I am still ready to hear your request. I'm just not yet clear about the basis for your request, or why you even think you should make one. Specifically, what do you think you did wrong when you lost your temper at the kids, so that you now seek forgiveness from me?*
Strong-willed adult:	You mean I didn't make you angry?
God:	*You just did it again.*
Strong-willed adult:	Did what?
God:	*Changed the subject instead of answering the question.*
Strong-willed adult:	Boy, you make things rough on me, just trying to make me bow

and scrape in contrition, eat crow and humble pie. All right, if you want that, I'll do it — sackcloth and ashes — the whole bit!

God: *Whoops! Mistaken identity.*

Strong-willed adult: Huh?

God: *You have just portrayed me as the kind of villain you considered your mother and father to be when you felt guilty around them.*

Strong-willed adult: I did?

God: *Didn't you always resent that about them? Didn't it seem to you that they mostly wanted you to suffer for the things you did that they didn't like? Didn't they work harder to prove themselves right than to help you learn principles from your mistakes, determinations that would help you to think your way through new situations you would face in the future?*

Strong-willed adult: Yeah, now that you mention it, I always did hate that about them.

God: *And now you approach me in the posture of a guilty wrongdoer, predicting that I will react in the same unkind way Mom and Dad did.*

Strong-willed adult: Well, you do react just like them.

God: *Only in your eyes. When you ask me to forgive you, and I ask you what you think you did wrong, you think I am kind of roasting you like your parents used to. Kind of making you stew in*

	your humiliation, prolonging your agony so I can feel like some kind of a victor over you. Right?
Strong-willed adult:	Yes, you said exactly what I think.
God:	*Fine, we agree on what **you** think I have done. Now, I will tell you how I see it. I, unlike your imperfect biological parents, whom I also love, respect your intellect, your opinions, and views. I talk with you in a way that calls forth the finest qualities I put in you when I designed you. I am interested in the results of your thinking. I truly look forward to comparing our views and showing you my ways, so you can consider them and see if you want to adopt them as your ways, by your own free choice.*
Strong-willed adult:	Hmm, what you say sounds good, but. . . .
God:	*But you doubt whether you can trust me yet, not to lose my temper at you?*
Strong-willed adult:	Right.
God:	*Does that give you any ideas about what might be wrong about your losing your temper at your kids?*

Empty Apologies

Do you ever hear an empty "I'm sorry"? The person means, "Please let me off the hook, even though I reserve the right to continue abusing you in the future." That person wants relief from the consequences of wronging you, but does not want to change the conditions that result in your hurt.

God hears these hollow pleas all the time. Note his policy

on them: "If we [freely] admit that we have sinned and confess our sins, He is faithful and just [true to His own nature and promises] and will forgive our sins [dismiss our lawlessness] and continuously cleanse us from all unrighteousness — everything not in conformity to His will in purpose, thought and action (1 John 1:9 AMPLIFIED).

God forgives us when we *confess*, not when we ask. Hear that again: the precondition for our forgiveness is not that we seek forgiveness, but that we confess our sins. The effective words are not, "I am sorry," but, "I did wrong." In fact, we even commit sin when we beg God to forgive us. We imply that we have to give him the idea or he won't think of it. We portray God as moody, sulky, and stubborn, requiring coaxing to get him to relent and let us off the hot seat.

The familiar Scripture, however, confirms to us that God has a forgiving nature. Like a firecracker, he just waits to go off with an explosion of joy. Our confession of wrongdoing lights the fuse. As soon as we admit our sin, he forgives us. If we add in there, "Please forgive me," we interrupt him, like pulling the trigger on a shotgun, feeling the recoil against the shoulder, and then saying, "I sure hope this thing goes off."

Full Apologies

Hand in glove with confessing goes the necessity of repenting, of turning around and going the other way. John the Baptist stressed the necessity and potency of rock-bottom repentance in my life, including, according to Luke 3:3–14: (a) clearsighted awareness of the ghastly awfulness of my wrongdoing, in the light of God's holy nature; (b) a feeling of abhorrence for my past wrongs; (c) utterly renouncing my past ways, in favor of (d) hearty commitment to specific, regular, and righteous conduct before God; and

(e) generous, fair, and gentle actions toward my fellow humans. I live a new life marked by my repeated choice to content myself with what I have in the way of earthly provisions, and to express appreciation and goodwill instead of griping.

Just as the processes of inhaling and exhaling use the same lungs, the process of repenting uses five A steps as does the process of forgiving.

Step One: *Acknowledge* My Wrongdoing

Get specific. Not just, "I blew my top at the kids," but, "I yelled at Susie and called her stupid. I pushed Jimmy and said I wanted him out of my sight. Then when my wife came in to calm me down, I swore at her and blamed her for the kids' misbehavior."

Viewing my own actions through the eyes of those I affect becomes the key to this step. Then I go to the persons I have offended and confess to them.

But how might I apply this first step to the larger issue of my strong-willed rebellion against God's authority? I would acknowledge: "God, I have conducted myself as if you were weak, stupid, and mean, instead of powerful, wise, and good. I have resented human authorities over me and have sought to defeat them when I did not like the way they led me. I have continued to use in adult life the maneuvers I learned as a strong-willed child. Thus, I have refused to respect any authority higher than my own."

Step Two: *Assess* the Impact

In the second step of repentance I *assess the impact* my actions and attitudes have had on others. Industrial corporations must file with the U.S. Government an environmental impact assessment for any major project they undertake, like building an electric power plant. We all share part of a spiritual ecology. What we do and say cannot help but have an impact on our fellow humans *and* on our Creator.

To properly assess that impact, I must relive it all in their shoes. Some examples:

> "I realize that I broke my mother's heart when I told her I didn't care what she thought, but that I intended to do what I wanted."

> "Constant complaining around my wife wrongly starves her of the encouragement that could lighten her load and brighten her enthusiasm for her God-ordained role as wife and mother."

> "By my stubbornness toward God, I have rebuffed the love that he stood ready to lavish upon me. I have done nothing less than fight against the very machinery by which the universe operates. I have cast my vote with those who murdered Jesus, when they said, 'We will not have this Man to rule over us.' "

Step Three: "*About* Face!"

Drill commanders bark out that order to a military company to head them 180 degrees opposite the direction they had been going. In Steps One and Two, I confess explicitly the ungodly aspects of my former direction. Now I tell what I would do differently if I had my past actions to do over again.

Genuine guilt reflects such a horror for what I have done to others that I would in no way repeat my offense if given the chance to do so again. What would I do instead?

"God, if I could go back to my teenage years with Mom, instead of breaking off from her for trying to dominate me, I would tell her I intend to obey her as the mother whom you put in authority over me. And I would tell her that she could make obedience easier for me, and more joyful also, if she took time to calmly explain the reasons behind the rules she laid down for me."

Step Four: *Anything* Else?

I don't want premature sutures over wounds I have not yet disinfected. I make sure to get all the poison out.

To this end I welcome criticism and other expressions of displeasure toward me from the persons I wronged. I sift it all like a prospector panning for gold in a mountain stream carefully washing away the lightweight gravel in order to leave behind the heavy, valuable nuggets. Anything I can remember from verbal attacks on me becomes priceless information about additional wrongs I need to confess and repent.

I also sift through my own remaining emotional discomfort about the event to detect any guilt indicating I probably did something else that I have not yet made right. I pay particular attention to any hurt, resentment, or bitterness I feel. I confess and repent of any wrong attitudes and actions on my part that I formerly justified by my perception that others treated me unfairly.

I consult third parties familiar with both me and the persons I wounded. I ask them anything they know about that I have not yet faced and dealt with regarding my misconduct. Once in junior high I learned from a third party the affection that a timid girl felt for me. So now I might learn from a messenger a lingering hurt that a timid victim still feels from me.

I do not rush the other person through the reconciliation. I take as my goal a felt unity between us, not merely my own relief from feeling in trouble. I want to heal it all.

Step Five: *Accountability*

Before my wife and I bought our house, we put down earnest money with the sellers. We thus showed our good-faith intention to proceed toward a concluded transaction. Our action indicated our willingness for it to cost us not to follow through with a promise we made. We, by our earnest money, protected the sellers against their potential loss of another buyer while they waited to see if we would make good on our promise.

When I seek to reconcile with someone I have wronged, by confessing and repenting, I ask that person to run a risk with me, namely the risk that I might hurt him or her in the same way again. Although I do not intend to hurt my victims again, for all they know, I could — and I need to offer them some protection at my expense.

One man found a creative way to safeguard his wife against his verbal tirades. He wanted no longer to blow up at her whenever she brought him bad news. So he suggested that whenever she fears he might blow up at something she tells him, she first warns him that she has such an item to tell. Then, when he asks her to tell him, she first gets a raw egg, holds it over his head, while telling him the bad news, and cracks it open if he blows up. In counseling they both joked about this shift of power to the underdog as "egg drop soup" for the husband, which kept the wife out of hot water! Of course, because they had this agreement, they never had to use it.

When my confession and repentance involve only a private sin that I have committed in my strong will against God, I make myself accountable to him for my future conduct by assigning a new role to my feelings. I convert guilt and resentment from my masters to my servants.

I now respect these feelings as warning signals God has

wired into me, like the red lights that automobile designers put into the dashboard of a car. When one goes on, I immediately speak to God as Father and say, "Oh, oh. Something's going on here that threatens to interfere with our close walk together. What am I doing to activate the signals?" God respects his children's intellect, and he jumps at the chance to sharpen my understanding and lead me ever deeper into those thoughts of his, which, before my repentance, could not become my thoughts. I thank him for creating a sensitive conscience in me.

What If I Don't *Feel* Forgiven?

Once I have taken the necessary steps to confess and repent, my final step remains to receive the forgiveness God so freely gives. But for the strong-willed person, that doesn't always come easy.

In her classic book, *The Christian's Secret of a Happy Life*, Hannah Whitall Smith quotes a strong-willed child who insisted that God does not forgive us immediately upon our confessing, but requires considerable suffering from us first. The child maintained, "I believe that *is* the way he does . . . no matter what the Bible says."

Like many strong-willed adults, that little girl would rather suffer by *her* timetable than accept forgiveness by God's. Her self put-down attempted to regulate God, since she preferred her own conclusions over God's authoritative promises. God says he forgives us when we confess and repent. Our lack of feeling forgiven reveals our posture of arguing against God.

The path to contentment and true self-acceptance lies in accepting God's contradiction of our ideas, welcoming his discipline, and acknowledging his terms for relating to him. He offers us much kinder terms than our own. At the same

time, we can seek to understand *why* God chooses to order
our lives the way he does. He *invites* our honest protests.

Consider Job, who expressed his suffering openly: "If I
called, and He answered me, yet would I not believe that
He listened to my voice" (Job 9:16 AMPLIFIED). What a strong-
willed flavor that statement has! His complaints resemble
the neurotic's reproaches against fate, life, and God. He
surely does not sound as if he *feels* forgiven.

But notice a different character to Job's words as he continues in his anguish: "I am weary of my life, *and* loathe it!
I will give free expression to my complaint; I will speak in
the bitterness of my soul. I will say to God, 'Do not condemn
me — do not make me guilty! Show me why You contend
with me' " (Job 10:1, 2 AMPLIFIED).

Perhaps Job's words serve as a model of honest wrestling
with God by an afflicted man who calls boldly for an encounter with the living God. We recognize Job's reverence
for God from the rest of his monologues. He doesn't deny
God's right to run the universe, as does the neurotic who
strives for the throne. Job asks for a response from God, not
an excuse or apology. Job wants more to understand than
to overrule God's ways.

Another biblical sufferer occasionally blurts out candid
displeasure toward God. By this honesty, he soon clears his
vision and remembers that God *is* God. In Psalm 10:1 he
protests:

Why, O LORD, do you stand far off? . . .

Then in verse 17 he finds a new perspective:

You hear, O LORD, the desire of the afflicted; . . .

Again in Psalm 13:1 he starts with:

> How long, O LORD? Will you forget me forever?
> How long will you hide your face from me?

Then in verse 6 his gloom dissolves in gratitude:

> I will sing to the LORD, for he has been good to me.

The psalmist's anger in relating to God differs from our wounded-pride anger, in which we want to break off relations with God. God has wired into us a way to gain perspective and relief. If we genuinely wrestle with him and candidly gripe to his face about how he treats us, the inevitable result becomes a meeting of the minds.

Starting off with, "God, you have *not* given me a conviction of your forgiveness," leads me on to the next logical statement: "God, you have shirked a portion of your duty toward me." That in turn leads me to say, "I am in a position to remind you of your obligations to me." That statement leads me further to tell God, "Just remember who's boss here."

That statement leads me to laughter that restores me to sanity, so that I end up saying like the psalmist:

> Great are you, O God, my LORD, and greatly to be praised, because you who owe me nothing have spared your hand from annihilating my insolent tongue, and in that great gesture of unmerited mercy toward me, have lavishly demonstrated your abundant forgiveness beyond all doubt.

Confessing, repenting, and accepting God's forgiveness launch us like newborn babes into a process of growth in that new area of life where we have freshly taken responsibility. How can we thereafter feed and exercise so as to develop into solid athletes of God?

9

Developing Spiritual Muscle

Imagine what would happen to a marathon runner who trained for a big race merely by eating the right foods. That runner would mistakenly emphasize only part of a truth: muscle tissue does need input of proper nutrition. However, healthy muscles require nourishment, rest, and *exercise* to attain fitness.

Spiritually, we have needs similar to muscles' needs. We need nourishment from our relationship with God. We need recognition from others. We also need rest in the form of occasional solitude. Most of all, we need exercise to keep us healthy and strong.

This chapter explores three kinds of spiritual exercise which can help us in our walk of faith and keep us from falling into the flabbiness of our old, strong-willed natures.

Exercising Generosity

My wife, Ruth, and I have moved six times during our married life. Each time Ruth quickly made new friends by asking her new neighbors in for coffee and a get-acquainted hour. As the newcomer, she reached out to the people who already lived there! She has heard other women talk about moves and how bruised they felt when they had to leave their friends. Then they moved into a new neighborhood and merely waited for people to approach them.

Ruth acts amazed when she hears these women complain about unfriendly neighborhoods. "How can any neighborhood be unfriendly if *you* are in it?" she asks. "How can you allow a neighborhood to stay unfriendly since you have it in your power to extend your friendship? And if one person, namely you, extends friendship, can anyone call the neighborhood 'unfriendly' anymore?"

It *is* more blessed to give than to receive, to be a host than a guest. "Blessed" means more rewarding, more personally satisfying, more fulfilling, more actively zesty. All of that comes to us more from generously dispensing what we have than it does from grasping for more or clutching to what we already have.

Recipes routinely require a pinch of salt because it brings out the unique flavor of each of the other ingredients. What does a pinch of *you* do for a recipe of family or friends? Jesus said you are the salt of the earth (Matt. 5:13). Note, not "you *should* be," not "try to be," but, "You *are* the salt of the earth." An intrusive ingredient in a recipe, salt's presence affects the whole meal. We choose what kind of influence to exert — to enhance or to pollute the recipe.

We do not just leak through life. We go about actively putting forward, flinging forth, ejecting, radiating a particular kind of influence, expression, or assertion. We bring nourishing or toxic effects, constructive contributions, or destructive diminutions into the lives of those around us.

Jesus offered constructive contributions wherever he went. Yet dubious, hostile, and even religious critics quizzed him

on his every move. One time they asked him why he con-
sorted with an ill-reputed crowd (Luke 5:30). They wondered
what he *got* out of associating with sinners. Jesus answered
in terms of what he *gave*. He mingled with others to contribute to their well-being; not to take selfish advantage of
their admiration to boost his own superiority. Unselfish love
for others motivated Jesus' actions.

The measure of generosity. The robes people wore in Jesus'
time served as more than just clothing. The bosom of a
robe formed a pouch, often used as a bag. With it, the
wearer could deliver and receive goods in bulk, such as
grain. It became the convenient Mediterranean measuring
cup. Jesus used it as an object lesson about generosity:
". . . For with the measure you deal out — that is, with the
measure you use when you confer benefits on others — it
will be measured back to you" (Luke 6:38 AMPLIFIED).

Jesus thus taught about the give and take of life. He
implied that we can enlarge our capacity only in the outgoing direction, the one *we* control. The extent to which we
stretch our pouch of generosity to others establishes the
maximum abundance we can later receive. Jesus applied
this principle particularly to generous forgiving, saying,
". . . acquit and forgive and release (give up resentment, let
it drop), and you will be acquitted and forgiven and re-
leased" (v. 37 AMPLIFIED).

See it with your mind's eye. Picture yourself wearing a
robe, size: extra-large. You use it as a pouch, at chest level,
to hold several pounds of moldy, smelly, bitter grain you
have kept far too long. At a beckoning from Jesus, you let
it drop. The robe falls flat against your skin. The rotten grain
falls to the ground. What a relief! Your arms can now freely
embrace that handsome, smiling Savior! Then you fluff your
robe into a large pouch, to take in his lavish outpouring of

the sweetest-tasting bread you've ever had — the Bread of Life.

Examples from the Master. Jesus repeatedly prescribed outgoing generosity as the heart of authentic living. In Luke 10, he advocated it from three different angles. First, he cited as the essence of the grand Hebrew tradition, descended from Moses, that we must love God and our neighbors heartily (v. 27).

Then Jesus told the Good Samaritan story with its clear moral: Align yourself with God's merciful heart and invest yourself to alleviate the conditions of people upon whom misfortunes have fallen through no lapse or laziness of their own.

Finally (Luke 10:38–42), the Master urged his friend, Martha, to involve herself more here and now with eternal matters than with material preparations. Like a wise and gentle daddy, he disarmed her self-imposed martyrdom. He lightheartedly rebuked Martha and praised the more leisurely, contemplative style of her sister, Mary.

Jesus confronted Martha with loving admonition. She had used the classic strong-willed gambit of harried busyness to extort approval from others, and she tried to coerce her sister to come under her command. She sought superiority through suffering; Jesus offered her partnership through participation.

No strings attached. Giving differs from contributing when it *obligates* the other person to receive. That type of giving is not more blessed than receiving. It actually becomes another form of receiving — a counterfeit generosity. It has a string attached, as does a payment in a deal which says, "Because I have been so kind to you, you are now duty-bound to show me your gratitude. You *owe* me appreciation. You *must* confess that I have done a wonderful deed."

Contributing means freely offering what I have, no strings

attached. I leave it as if deposited in God's hands, for him to do with as he sees fit. I trust him with it as God of the harvest, free to multiply a hundredfold, or to parch the seedlings in a summer drought.

Jesus knew the unthinkable catastrophe in the life of the rich, young ruler who dabbled in spiritual interests. He prescribed for that fellow (not necessarily for everyone else): ". . . go, sell your possessions and give to the poor, and you will have treasure in heaven. Then come, follow me" (Matthew 19:21). We can see that young man's face blanch, his jaw drop, and his shoulders droop. "What? Face life without my financial security blanket? Suffer the shocks of life without a credit-card cushion? I couldn't stand it."

Note that Jesus did not lay this heavy confrontation on this wealthy man uninvited. The man had asked what he could do to belong to the exquisite assembly of like-minded people who thrill to the presence of God through all eternity. The Savior leaked a secret: heaven's inhabitants have in common an investing mentality. They take initiative to benefit their fellow humans.

Practicing Self-Denial

Contributing to others presupposes the spiritual exercise of self-denial. Imagine a hungry farmer in the spring of the year looking at his supply of grain. He thinks about how good it would feel to eat it. But he says, "No, my family and I will skimp and go hungry for a while longer. I am going to take that seed and give it away to the ground."

The farmer's family could easily make that good grain into bread and eat it right now, to satisfy a temporary hunger. Instead, the farmer plants it in the ground, with no guarantee of what will happen to it. It has died as far as he is concerned. He cooperates with God by trusting him for a harvest.

Only by that way of self-denial does the farmer stand any chance of a future free of hunger. The walk of faith involves giving away that which we tend to cling to, as our part in working with God's promise to multiply it.

Jesus had a rather pithy way of inviting followers. He did not make it easy. He made it possible for everyone, yet evidently did not expect his criteria to meet with a majority response. Note how he clearly made it optional:

> If any person wills to come after Me, let him deny himself — that is, disown himself, forget, lose sight of himself and his own interests, refuse and give up himself — and take up his cross daily, and follow Me [that is, cleave steadfastly to Me, conform wholly to My example, in living and if need be in dying also].
>
> For whoever would preserve his life and save it, will lose and destroy it; but whoever loses his life for My sake, he will preserve and save it [from the penalty of eternal death] (Luke 9:23, 24 AMPLIFIED).

The differentness of the way of Jesus. Anyone who chooses to go the way of Jesus finds that His way goes precisely against the human inclination to seek superiority as protection against bruises to self-esteem. His way denies one's own status. More than that, His way refuses even the effort to feed and protect one's prestige. Instead, the disciple walks daily into the face of humiliation if that becomes necessary to contribute to the kingdom of God.

Take up his cross daily. Think what that means. People get killed on crosses. Worse than that, they suffer intensely for a long time before they die on their crosses. Worse yet, before the spikes enter their flesh, they suffer the searing scorn of onlookers who watch them drag their own instrument of torture and death to the place of execution. They are forced against their wills to perform that most degrading duty, as public proof of their identity as defeated, impotent, hated, rejected, worthless nonmembers removed from society.

Jesus taught *that* as a manageable way to live. Doing worthwhile kingdom work impressed him more than did the horrors of humiliation. He knew he would soon face the fate we all fear worse than death — rejection. He clearly decided he would not diminish his own ongoing work for the kingdom, even though the very authorities with whom he most eagerly wanted fellowship despised him for it.

Remember, some of the religious men who called for his crucifixion had probably sat in on those exhilarating conversations he had enjoyed for several days in Jerusalem at age twelve. How he would have loved their approval now — but he denied himself and took up his cross. He asks *of* us what he willingly did *for* us.

With less than twenty-four hours to live, Jesus agonized with God in the Garden of Gethsemane (Luke 22:42–44). His intense praying showed mature, manly revulsion, of which tantrums make a childish counterfeit. Jesus earnestly implored God against the task he perceived God laying before him.

Jesus beseeched God to remove the cup of death from him — a very human request. If God had another way to accomplish his purpose, Jesus wanted it. Yet God told him, "No!" There was no other way. And Jesus accepted the answer, maintained his contact with God, and furthermore affirmed God's plan as the one that would ultimately prevail.

Taking "no" for an answer. The body of Christ in America

today suffers from a nutritional deficiency. We lack the trace elements contained in the fruit of the Spirit called "long-suffering." We overindulge on the junk food of short-suffering. We need to become familiar with *not* getting some of what we urgently want. We need to follow Jesus' example and practice taking *no* for an answer.

The mature adult, like Jesus, in the role of subordinate, appeals vigorously to God to modify the orders. Always behind the subordinate's bold, emphatic request resounds willingness for God's *no* to stand as the final and the finest answer. By contrast, strong-willed protests carry the threat that we will break off relations with God if we don't get our way. We thus reveal, as the ultimate authority that guides us, our own willful desire.

Note the remarkable calm with which Jesus faced the mockery and abuse that came just hours after his impassioned praying. He obviously didn't just go along resentfully with the *no* from God, thinking it a stupid and unfair answer. Instead, he had settled something with God in the Garden. He heard more than just, "No, you can't have your way." He recognized that his powerful, wise, and good Father had said, "No, I have something far more splendid in mind for you than just freedom from pain." And so Jesus, for that unseen joy set before him, endured the cross, ignoring its shame (Heb. 12:2).

Encounters with nature. God has designed our natural environment as one of his favorite kindergartens for training us. Bible stories tell of wilderness experiences where men of God grew in wisdom and maturity. With no one else around to pamper us, we can encounter God's laws of nature as a perfectly consistent parent. At the age of thirty-eight, I went on a stress-camping expedition in the wilderness, and there watched God tame a large portion of my childish strong will.

As I look back on that profound experience, I see God as my skilled psychotherapist, maneuvering me into an uncomfortable situation that I could get out of only by doing something mature and responsible. I entered a tender trap in which I would be blessed if I complied and blessed if I defied — the opposite of damned-if-I-did-and-damned-if-I-didn't.

I had sore muscles. I felt tired and hungry, dirty, and thirsty. Bugs droned relentlessly around my head. My repellent did not work against them. The monotony of day-after-day backpacking on miles and miles of tedious trails bored me. I hated it. No, that's too mild. I *vowed* my hatred of the program.

I decided I had made a dumb mistake in coming on the trip. I wanted to quit. I felt the same futile frustration I remembered as a kid when I did poorly at a game and wanted to take my bat and ball and go home. The problem dated back to my past, when I could always get out of hated situations one way or another. I could always quit or get an easier assignment. When I had sought special treatment in the past, the answer had always come back *yes*. Now I faced *no*, and it aroused all my stubborn fury at not holding the driver's seat.

I found myself in the heart of a remote forest, arduous miles from the highways that could get me to the comforts of home. I had only three options for getting out: (1) following the program as planned; (2) making the other four group members carry me; (3) suicide. In good psychotherapy at a time of depression years before, I had decided I would never take my own life. That left only two options open to me.

If I fell helpless, or sick, or otherwise passive, I probably could induce the others to carry my gear and me out of the woods. However, that meant I would have to trust them —

one of my strong-willed hang-ups. I preferred to do things *my* way. I would not leave myself at the mercy of anyone else's competence. If I chose option two, I would have to rely on my group's power, wisdom, and goodness. God could use my passivity to break my strong will against trusting others.

I could choose the first option and walk out of the woods on my own power, as the wilderness seminar required. I knew I *could* do that; I just didn't *want* to. It galled me to realize that I had gotten wedged into a corner where the easiest thing for me to do was the one I hated most to do: obey the rules of an authority I didn't want to follow.

I felt defeated, humiliated, broken. Tantrum anger, my most valued ally, proved useless to me in this pickle. The distance to go exceeded what I could make by a temporary adrenalin surge of anger. I finally had to admit that I had encountered a situation bigger than myself.

I had to depend on forces I could not control: my body's metabolism of the food our leaders rationed out; my companions' work in preparing campsites and meals, trail markers and maps made by someone else. My sovereignty consisted of two menial functions: lifting my weary legs one at a time, and heaving my lungs breath upon breath.

I now look back upon that onerous ordeal as one of the most valuable experiences of my life. I benefited from it in direct proportion to how savagely I hated it *and did it anyway*! I demanded that God give me an easy way out of the woods. He said *no*. I took *no* for my answer, and grew several inches in spiritual stature. I learned to bend to a will higher than my own.

I had acted like a stiff patient, coming with atrophied muscles to a physical therapist. God, my Great Therapist, showed kindness in making me bend my inner muscles no matter how painful. I now have a range of movement I never knew before.

Fasting to Exercise Spiritual Muscles

We can discipline ourselves by refusing food occasionally for a period of time. I know one godly teacher who advocates missing breakfast and lunch each Wednesday and Friday, and praying frequently during those hours for spiritual revival in our nation.

An obvious caution with fasting: don't substitute credit for calories. We do not discipline ourselves if, while abstaining from food, we let people know about it, so that they can admire our show of righteousness. Then we merely replace one indulgence with another, and allow ourselves to remain spiritually flabby.

I have learned something about the value of fasting along with prayer. While praying, I work to maintain the realistic attitude that God runs his universe competently, and that I invest time and energy in prayer so that he can change *me*. This attitude of obedient openness to God normally results in my recognition of his nudging me to let go of something I have unwittingly clutched close. Then he can fill my hands with a new treasure. The old things I cling to usually include *my* idea of how to handle a certain task, *my* idea of the best way for me to use my time ... *my* preference, *my* desire, *my* opinion, *my* dream.

Some years ago, our church congregation fasted and prayed for a week, seeking God's guidance in the matter of expanding our facilities. I could easily pray the wrong way: "God, please change the minds of these stubborn people around me, and help them to see the wisdom and correctness of the solution I have in mind for this problem." God does not honor that prayer, but instead pressures me to open my mind, to hear and consider the proposals of others. To obey him, I need to let go of my narrow-minded insistence that I am right. As I let go, I die to myself by giving up my pride.

Fasting can help this death-to-self process. My life without food for a period of time shows me a parable of "letting go." Fasting gives me an active way to say to myself, "I can do without something important to me." Thus, I make it easier for me to cooperate with God's initiative, which requires me to let go of my own way. Fasting becomes something I do for me, not for God. I specifically use fasting to tune myself to notice and respond to God's prompting.

The hunger pangs I feel while fasting give me a parable about seeking God's ways. I hunger and thirst after righteousness. I want to refer to food and water like psalmists did, as examples of desirable gifts from God. My pangs cry out, "Oh, God, as food satisfies the hunger of my craving body, so does your wisdom satisfy the craving in my inner being."

I just recently recognized the personal benefit of fasting. In the past, when I read in the Bible of people praying and fasting, I wrote it off as an ancient custom, along with sackcloth and ashes. If I pictured myself fasting at all, I regarded it as a sacrifice I would make in order to twist God's arm.

We all tend to abuse godly disciplines, to try to manipulate God by our sacrifices. We offer such sacrifices as dues payments to God to get him into our debt so that he *has* to grant our requests. Sacrifice in this spirit connotes rebellion; we dictate to God how he shall respond to our prayers. We compete with God himself.

I do myself a favor when I fast and pray in earnest. I allow my body to remind me continually that I can approach God only on his terms. I remind myself that I am willing to give up anything precious to me in order to experience the surpassing excellence of knowing his wisdom and his ways.

Having developed spiritual muscle, by exercising generosity, practicing self-denial, and fasting, we become eager to use it against one of our lifelong enemies — fear.

10

Facing the Bogeyman

Suppose you could go back to one nightmare-ridden night of your childhood. You find yourself trembling in your bed in almost pitch-darkness. Only a trickle of light leaks around the covering over your window. You notice a movement in the darkest part of the room. A humpy hulk you have seen before looms eerily. In the past you have always managed to send him away in the nick of time by a light or a mom summoned to shoo the bogeyman. This time you decide to face him fully, come what may. Sure you shiver, but you decide not to let your fear hold you back. You act, even though afraid. You say, "Hey, you, bogeyman. I'm over here. Come right here where I can see you."

He snarls and lumbers over to you, hoping to scare you under the covers. Instead you get out of bed and stand on the floor to meet him head-on. He shuffles right up to you, growling his foul breath into your face. You stretch your neck forward even farther to get a completely detailed view of that fiendish face in the faint light. And wouldn't you know it, he has acne! Bad case of it! No wonder he acts the way he does. He has to scare people off so they won't see him up close. He couldn't bear the embarrassment.

But now you know his long-held secret. You have him at your mercy. How do you plan to use your power over him? Will you, too, laugh at him as did the others who hurt him long ago? You think of it for a moment. Then your heart melts. You ruffle his hair with one hand, then say, "Well, we've both had a hard night. What do you say we get some shut-eye, partner?" Then you crawl back into your bed, and he to his corner, and you both get a long-sought night's rest.

Cartoonist Gary Larson depicts bogeymen afraid of real people in the bedroom scene below.

Doing the Feared Thing

When we deliberately face what we normally avoid, we become different. Facing our fears acts as another muscle-building technique, one of the most powerful around.

Many of our human fears stem from pride. Fearful "I can't stand it" translates into prideful "I won't stand for it."

What happens to us in situations we truly cannot stand? We keel over. For example, we cannot stand a lack of oxygen for more than a matter of seconds without passing out. Instead of remaining on our feet, we fall down.

But when we say, "I can't stand it," we do not usually mean we will physically faint or die if the current stress continues upon us. We really mean that we don't like it. We would rather not bear it. We find it more than we prefer to endure. Our strong will comes in here. In our prideful pretentions to the throne we believe we should not have to tolerate what we do not like. We consider ourselves entitled to exemption from exertion.

"I've got it again, Larry . . . an eerie feeling like there's something on top of the bed."

You can shatter the ice of your own pride by deliberately doing something worthwhile that you fear. For instance, if you have been shy, pray in public. If you have resented your parents, or feared their domination, hug them. As you do so, see yourself pulling the fuse out of a bomb labeled "I CAN'T STAND IT".

One of the things we think we "can't stand" is disapproval. Some people so fear disapproval that they treat it like a vicious vampire bat that could drain their life's blood. Jesus regarded disapproval as more like a mosquito. He recognized that it can only buzz around. At worst, it can give a minor sting — more an inconvenience than a terror.

Jesus often met with disapproval. One day he provoked it by arranging dinner at the home of Jericho's Public Enemy Number One, Zacchaeus, the crooked, treasonous tax collector (Luke 19:1–10).

Jesus, the famous and popular wonderworker, faced complaints against the work he considered right. Since he did not have immunity to disapproval, we probably cannot expect to have it either. The treatment we happen to get at the moment from the crowd at hand does not always accurately reflect our worth to the human race or the kingdom of God.

An act of cowardice by a Roman official allowed the illegal execution of Jesus, the Messiah (Matt. 27:24). Pilate caved in to fear of rejection; Jesus did not. We do no small thing when we stand courageously for what we regard as right. Every time we hold firm against intimidation, and exercise authority for a just and righteous outcome, we correct part of an error that cost Jesus his life. We help to set the human order straight. Not that we undo Pilate's wrong, but we validate the rightness of what he should have done.

Building Boldness

How do we get the kind of boldness this action requires? Part of the secret lies in exchanging one place of security for another. Peter discovered this one day on the Sea of Galilee, when he saw Jesus walking on the sea toward the boat and asked to join him. Peter walked briefly on the water himself, then began to sink (Matt. 14:30).

Peter's walk shows what we all experience in growing up spiritually. He had two places of security, and a solitary journey stretched between them. He wanted to leave the old, familiar security of the smelly fishing boat for the new, thrilling security of companionship with his Master, Jesus. But between the two he wrestled alone. His feet had to take those steps; Jesus would not do it for him. Peter had asked Jesus to beckon him. Jesus had said, "Come," not, "Here, I'll do it for you."

Peter felt the wind and mistakenly took the attitude that circumstances could overwhelm him. "I can't stand it" shows the childish way of thinking in all of us that shuts down our bold use of the abilities God has delegated to us to handle our circumstances. We begin to move toward our attractive companion, Jesus. At the same time, we hesitate to leave the familiar, childish, symptomatic ways of coping with life that have afforded us *some* advantages in the past. When we launch out and find ourselves in the wind of adversity, we need not yield to our neurotic anxiety. We do not have to agree with Satan's lie that we "can't stand it."

No question about it: God's way for us, his way of growth, always has with it the temporary, lonely journey through buffeting circumstances. Faith means bold action when we do not feel secure. Courage means going ahead even though scared.

The Arrogance of Worry

When we dread some coming event, it shows that we are thinking in terms of mustering up sufficient power within ourselves to handle the task alone. Scripture teaches us that every ripple of energy we ever expend comes to us as a gift from God, in whom we live and move and have our being. In fretting, we snub that power source and look to our own resources. The Bible calls that "works," and says that we do it in order to boast.

So, worry is a form of boasting! When we act as if we *should* be able to handle something without God's empowerment, we imply that we *can.* The serpent's lie from the Garden of Eden still appeals to us: "You will be like God — *if* you take matters into your own hands."

The misuse of responsibility. Someone has defined worry as taking on a responsibility that God never intended us to have. Sometimes people use fear in the opposite way, to avoid ordinary tasks and their consequences. They follow the motto: "Nothing ventured, nothing lost." They thus refuse to inch the human enterprise forward by venturing for the possibility of gain. Phobias represent an across-the-board way to avoid venturing. An agoraphobic woman, for example, who does not leave her house, certainly avoids doing anything blameworthy or embarrassing in public.

One woman used several phobias as excuses for saying *no* to certain activities. She did not want to say *no* outright in words, because she equated it with loud, out-of-control anger that she feared she might lapse into if she ever let herself express candid refusal. She lived by the absurd notion, "The world is too fragile to survive the full force of my fury if I let it loose."

An overly conscientious male client obsessed and fretted over the possibility that his wife might leave him as his mother had left his father years earlier. He still felt responsible for that breakup of his childhood family. "It was something about me that I didn't do right," he insisted as we discussed why his mother left. He *wanted* to regard it as his fault, because then he could cling to the belief that it came under his control, and therefore he could prevent Mom from leaving. His self-condemnation provided him a feeling of protection against vulnerable dependency on the integrity of loved ones.

An Antifear First-Aid Kit

An obsessive mother could hardly get out of her head the thought that, if she picked up a butcher knife at home, she might stab her baby son with it. She changed that obsession by putting it to work. Every time that automatic thought came to her, she deliberately pictured herself instead doing something positive *for* her son (like rubbing his body with a soothing lotion while humming to him), and a second positive thing *with* the knife (like slicing watermelon).

When you fearfully ask yourself "What if...?" proceed consciously and deliberately to answer the question with a series of the worst outcomes you can imagine. Then enumerate three benefits within each one of those tragedies. Find something you can like about every outcome that you do not like. Many of the horrors you imagine will consist of losses (death of a loved one, loss of your own health or property or status in life). And every loss carries a built-in benefit: it frees you for a new attachment, with new experiences and memories you could not have had if the former good situation stayed the same.

Do an energy conversion. An electrical powerhouse converts the energy of heat into the energy of motion, and that into the energy of electricity. Convert fear into enthusiasm. Both grow from a common root called *excitement* or *arousal*. You can just plain deliberately say, "I can hardly wait for X!" where X represents something you fear and prefer to avoid. Find some aspect about X that you can genuinely welcome, if only the chance to see what it's like.

Put worry to work. Use each occasion of dread as a reminder to take one small, constructive step. A salesman,

worried about slow business, decided to use each awareness of worry as a signal to set one lunch appointment with
a potential business contact. A mother, fretting about her
teenage son out late with the car, chose to let each furrow-
ing of her brow trigger into thanking God for one specific
excellent memory from the sixteen good years she already
had with her son.

God does not give us fears; he offers peace instead. So,
Satan, our adversary, entices us to worry. He hates it when
we praise the majesty of God and adore Christ as Lord. So,
if we make our worries reminders to praise the Lord, Satan
soon forsakes his promotion of worry in us. Say aloud in
your mind when you realize you are worrying, "Ah, thank
you, Satan, for reminding me to praise my wonderful Lord
Jesus Christ." Then tell Jesus that he is the excellent King
of kings and Lord of lords.

Use worries as windows into your soul. Whatever you
worry about losing may constitute an idol that you worship
more devotedly than you do the living God. If you worry
about looking foolish in front of other people, then you fear
losing their admiration. Proper concern to show common
courtesy carries with it no compulsion. When you desperately *must* assure yourself that people think well of you, then
let your anguish tip you off to your pagan worship of created
things rather than the Creator.

Instead of trying to *stop* your fearing, redirect it. Turn that
energy of worship back to its rightful object. See a terrifying
picture of yourself powerless before an overwhelming dis-
play of God's destructive power, from which he spares you,
at his mere pleasure, with no obligation to you to do so.
For example, picture yourself walking up a mountainside
gully between steep, unclimbable walls. Suddenly, down the
gully toward you thunders a furious avalanche of boulders
twice your size. As they come to you, each one skims past

your body a hair's breadth away, leaving you untouched. Deliberately turn your fearful tendencies toward the constructive project of developing within yourself that awesome fear of the Lord that gives you wisdom.

Rethink the unthinkable. Many people fear loud, angry voices from loved ones. They live by mottoes like "Peace at any price" and "Don't rock the boat." Strong-willed adults or children in their lives too easily dominate them by threatening to get mad. These fearful people chose, in a forgotten moment in childhood, to regard raised voices as "intolerable." In counseling I ask them to bring the matter up for a vote again in their soul's inner congress. "This time," I urge, "relabel loud voices as 'unpleasant,' and decide to tolerate them rather than avoid them at the cost of suppressing your own opinion around someone who disagrees with you."

A Picture of Security

You misplace your fears. You show greater awe for your bogeyman than for God. God alone deserves your fear. He alone controls your heartbeat at his whim. A mere puff of his breath could snuff the flickering candle flame of your life before you draw your next breath freely from his vast ocean of air. He and none other keeps your fragile planet in orbit and on axis and in one piece. He holds you and your eternal destiny in his hands, with or without your permission, whether you like it or not.

Think of yourself as a frightened nonswimmer clinging desperately to a life raft in the Pacific Ocean. You refuse to leave your security, even to board the luxury liner that has just pulled up alongisde you. But may Captain Jesus have your permission to hoist you, in your raft, into the shallow swimming pool aboard the ship?

Several decades after Jesus walked on the stormy water

of the Sea of Galilee, an eyewitness calmly retold the story. That writer quoted Christ's emphatic antidote for fear: "It is I; be not afraid! — I AM; stop being frightened!" (John 6:20 AMPLIFIED).

We can employ fear as emotional energy available to get information about unfamiliar situations we cannot avoid. Jesus responded to that information hunger in his frightened disciples by offering the fundamental fact that makes everything else make sense: "I AM." It was Jehovah's declaration of being to Moses (Exod. 3:14). On the basis of his existence Christ offers us the option to *fear not* in any situation.

God exists! More than that, God personally *declares* to us, for our relief and benefit, that he exists *and* that he rules. He stands ready to use his power to caress, heal, nourish, cuddle, and comfort us. We remain secure *only* in those magnificent hands that could crush us, for they belong to Jesus, who stared the bogeyman in the face through Good Friday, then put him in the grave on Easter.

Part Three

How to Live with a Strong-Willed Adult

11

More Than Conquerors

Linda's husband, Larry, paid her several sarcastic "compliments" at a party one evening in front of others: "That dress looks nice on you, Linda. It should — you paid enough for it. Besides, it covers up your middle-aged spread fairly well."

Linda waited until after the party, then told Larry alone, "I felt hurt when you made sarcastic remarks to me in front of others, and I would like you to promise me that from now on in public you will only speak well of me."

Larry blew up. "You're always criticizing me. I can't say the slightest thing without offending you. When are you going to grow up?"

Linda remembered a principle she had recently learned from a book she read about marital communication skills. Having aroused Larry's emotions by her appropriately confrontive "I felt hurt . . ." message, she next shifted gears into sympathetically listening to his answers. She responded, "I guess you feel attacked by what I'm saying. You probably feel picked on, as if I don't give you a break."

Larry snarled caustically, "Oh, so now you're the big psychologist, using your marvelous listening skills. You really think you're pretty great, don't you?"

Linda did not know what to do next. She had gone by the book, showing good faith to Larry by seeking to understand his feelings as well as to help him understand hers. She had kept a friendly attitude, without any argumentative tone in her voice. But Larry did not respond according to the book. He handcuffed her by his blustering approach and his rebuff of her attempt to understand his feelings. She could see only three options open to her: (1) quit complaining and merely endure Larry's continued rudeness like a worthless prisoner; (2) divorce Larry; or (3) use threats and other power tactics to *force* Larry to treat her kindly. She welcomed the chance to learn a fourth path open to her in counseling.

How to Recognize a Strong-Willed Loved One

When I describe strong-willed children, I generally emphasize their opposition to authority. This often shows up as passive refusal to do what the rules require. When I talk about strong-willed adults as people to live with, however, I refer to more actively abusive, unkind persons who seem unresponsive to requests for greater thoughtfulness. They interpret such requests as condemnations. They are allergic to blame. They sense it in the slightest comment to the effect that they might consider changing the way they have done something. They come across as hypersensitive to rejection, and interpret innocuous events as ridicule. Such persons are sometimes called "irregular people."

These irregular people live by the motto "The best defense is a strong offense." Considering themselves always vulnerable to attacks for displeasing a loved one, they maintain a stance of aggressive attack toward the loved one. They nitpick perfectionistically, constantly finding fault. They insist that the loved one do things *their* way. They major in controlling others by angrily intimidating or by cleverly inducing guilt feelings in them.

They do not share conversations but orchestrate them. They have an uncanny knack of making you look like *you're* the crazy one. They ask your point of view, not to consider it, but to demolish it. They *must* be right, regardless of the cost to their relationships.

Many clients who come to me for counseling speak of a demanding, critical, unappreciative, older parent as the strong-willed person in their lives. Others present themselves as the spouses of alcoholics, physical abusers, and manic-depressives in manic episodes.

This chapter aims to offer some of the wisdom sought in the Serenity Prayer:

> God grant me the serenity
> To accept the things I cannot change,
> Courage to change the things I can,
> And wisdom to know the difference.

that is, to know the difference between things we can change and things we cannot. It seeks to induce and equip readers not to *win* power struggles but to *end* them.

The Key for You

Al-Anon, the self-help group for loved ones of alcoholics, urges its members to give up all attempts to stop the alcoholic from drinking and concentrate instead on changing themselves, correcting their own wrongs and promoting their own maturity. They say, "Quit trying to manipulate your alcoholic into Alcoholics Anonymous [AA], and you yourself follow the Twelve Steps to spiritual growth that AA teaches, beginning with admitting that you are powerless over the alcoholic's drinking and that your own life has become unmanageable in your obsession to manage the alcoholic."

The Twelve Steps

1. We admitted we were powerless over alcohol — that our lives had become unmanageable.
2. Came to believe that a Power greater than ourselves could restore us to sanity.
3. Made a decision to turn our will and our lives over to the care of God as we understood Him.
4. Made a searching and fearless moral inventory of ourselves.
5. Admitted to God, to ourselves and to another human being the exact nature of our wrongs.
6. Were entirely ready to have God remove all these defects of character.
7. Humbly asked Him to remove our shortcomings.
8. Made a list of all persons we had harmed and became willing to make amends to them all.
9. Made direct amends to such people wherever possible except when to do so would injure them or others.
10. Continued to take personal inventory and when we were wrong, promptly admitted it.
11. Sought through prayer and meditation to improve our conscious contact with God as we understood Him, praying only for knowledge of His will for us and the power to carry that out.
12. Having had a spiritual awakening as the result of these steps, we tried to carry this message to others, and to practice these principles in all our affairs.

When we become impatient with how a loved one fails to act responsibly toward us, we tend to take on the role of enforcer, trying to coerce the wrongdoer into treating us properly. We tend to become vigilantes, taking law enforcement into our own hands. Feelings of resentment within us give us a sure sign that we have given up on God's government and asserted our own.

"Why should this happen to *me*?" sounds like a question, but really registers a strong-willed rebel's protest. Nevertheless, repeating it slowly, as a serious question, can suggest fresh approaches to a stale situation.

The biblical view. Genesis, the book of beginnings, ends with a focus on the wisdom and godly character of a man badly abused by several loved ones. Joseph expressed his peace of mind toward his strong-willed brothers in this pithy philosophy: the very actions that they intended for evil against him, God intended for good.

The Bible teaches a three-dimensional perspective — not I-versus-you, but I and you both on assignment from and individually accountable to a power and authority greater than either of us.

Some sixteen hundred years after the time of Joseph, one follower of Jesus asked about another, "Lord, what about him?" (John 21:21). How utterly like us when we see someone else getting by with wrong behavior at our expense. How insistently we press that question when advised to attend to our own responsibilities and stop trying to change the strong-willed tormentors in our lives. And how does Jesus answer that question, to his disciples today as surely as to the nosey one back then? ". . . what is that to you? You must follow me."

When God chose to become a man, he took the vocation of carpenter. He still uses abrasive circumstances in the lives of his loved ones to rub off their rough edges. *See your irregular person as God's sandpaper.*

Look for *God's* purposes in allowing that strong-willed loved one in your life. Let go of your demand for better treatment and seize the opportunity to become a better person. View the strong-willed person as a hireling of God assigned to place obstacles in your life that will exercise you in ways you would never seek but that will make you a muscular athlete in the spiritual arena.

Return to your serious question, "Why should this injustice happen to me?" Imagine God whispering his answer to you: "Because you need exactly the kind of workout provided by that piece of gym equipment. You are weak and flabby in a certain set of muscles that I need to use in my future plans for you."

Forsake these old rebel yells. "Why should I have to be the one to do all the changing?" If you feel this objection arising in you at the admonition to concentrate on *your* change, recognize that you have your gaze on what the other person is doing, rather than on what development God wants to work in you. Stop keeping score. Take *your* assignment from God and let God deal with your loved one as *he* sees fit.

Still feel uneasy as you consider doing that? Perhaps you think like the Al-Anon member who came to me saying that she knew the slogan LET GO AND LET GOD, but she wasn't quite sure that she could trust God to do things right if she let him run her situations his way. I suggested to her a slight addition to the slogan, to really bring out her willingness to trust God regardless. I wrote for her on my business card: LET GO AND LET GOD GOOF!

Do you sometimes reject advice with words like, "Have you ever had to live with someone who . . . ?" Do you hear what you are saying behind that challenge? "Show me your credentials, and I will discredit them. If you realized fully enough how unusually badly and unfairly I have suffered, you would have to agree with the hopeless conclusion I have come to."

Do people ever hear you grumble about your situation, "All I ask is a little ..."? Notice how that statement translates: "Since my request is so small, it's okay for me to order God and others to grant it."

Have you ever heard yourself say that you have already gone the second mile with your difficult person? If so, you may have walked two miles, but you do not know what Jesus meant when he taught, "Do not resist an evil person. If someone strikes you on the right cheek, turn to him the other also ... If someone forces you to go one mile, go with him two miles" (Matt. 5:39, 41).

Jesus recommended positive initiative in place of automatic reflex. Notice he said, "Do not *resist*"; he did not say, "Give in to." He taught his listeners to actively do something other than resist. The man who strikes you on one cheek expects and prepares himself for a retaliatory slap from you. He thus proposes an agenda of conflict. When you instead turn to him your unbruised cheek, you propose a novel, surprising agenda of goodwill. When you cheerfully walk a second mile after the required one, you propose a relationship based on generous cooperation, rather than on tit-for-tat obligation and competition. You demonstrate that *you*, not the other person, determine how far you walk.

"Believe me, I've gone the second mile" generally means that you grudgingly paid some sort of emotional dues for which you expect repayment. That's the old game that your tormentor proposes. Leave it and propose the new one that wishes well and does not keep score. Take delight in behaving decently. Exult in a victory over your greatest enemy — your own strong will.

If you continue the power struggle with your strong-willed

loved one, you may win. In that case you can clutch to yourself the lonely title of "Conqueror." But if you forsake your impulse to pursue that victory and instead initiate a new way of relating that benefits both you and your loved one, then you defeat a deadly situation that threatens to strangle you both. You hold the Medal of Honor in God's army, bearing the inscription MORE THAN CONQUEROR.

Your Love Displaces Your Fear

Burn victims. In her junior year of college, my wife, Ruth, severely burned her face and hands in a kitchen accident. One chilly evening on a date six months later, we entered a room with a cozy fire crackling in a fireplace at its far end. Ruth instantly spun around and cried, "The fire. It's too much. It hurts my face and hands!"

No visible scars remained, but extreme sensitivity to the original hurt carried into the new, healthy skin. Ruth could feel infrared radiation at levels much below my ability to detect it. Now as counselors we see among strong-willed persons who make themselves hard to live with, the same kind of exquisite overreaction to trifling emotional heat. As we often say of persons who have suffered rejection or betrayal, "They've been burned."

Childhood napalm. Remember Linda and her strong-willed husband, Larry, who insulted her at parties? Well, Larry kept it up, and Linda became more and more emotionally distant from him. A friend once tried to reconcile them. Each had expressed to this friend love for the other and a desire to reconcile.

The friend told Larry that Linda would easily melt and feel deeply loved if Larry would tell her, in person or by letter, that he realized he had hurt her by his loud voice and unkind words, that he was sorry, and that he would not mistreat her in the future.

Larry reacted strongly against that suggestion, vowing he would never "kowtow" to Linda. The friend pressed: why would Larry consider his apology to Linda abject humiliation, rather than an act of manly leadership? Larry said that, as a kid, his older brother used to try to boss him by verbally demanding that Larry admit he was wrong and his brother was right. "And," Larry told his friend emphatically, "I would deny him his victory."

In his childhood situation, Larry came to view life in a way that regarded any confession of error on his part as a mortal defeat that gave the other person inordinate power to debase him. Even agreeing to go with Linda to marriage counseling seemed to Larry like a confession of wrong or weakness or need. So his particular kind of crippling kept him from the treatment that could heal it. There in a sentence lies the heartrending tragedy of the strong-willed adult.

Perfected love. If you feel flickers of compassion for Larry, you are plugging into the power source that can dispel your own enslaving emotional reactions toward your irregular loved one. The aging apostle John put it this way: ". . . full-grown (complete, perfect) love turns fear out of doors and expels every trace of terror!" (1 John 4:18 AMPLIFIED). The traces of terror include your hurt feelings, resentments, guilt, and hostility, because all derive from fear of the fate worse than death — exclusion.

Compassion so engrosses us with caring for the needs of the wounded, bleeding, sobbing, lonely other person that we forget to wonder what that person thinks of us. We lose ourselves in generous preoccupation with the project of feeding a starving person. In this frame of mind, we do not question our own "in-ness"; we *exercise* it!

The perfected, mature love *by* us that casts out fear *in* us takes the form of compassion. Compassion displaces fear. The two cannot live together in one mind at the same time anymore than a basketball and a bowling ball can occupy one hand at the same time. In holding one, we drop the other. Seeing our strong-willed loved ones as limping, suffering, lonely, handicapped orphans behind grotesque Halloween masks gives us much more of a one-another large heart toward them than when we see them as poised, confident, malicious devils bent on our destruction. Sure they are unpleasantly defensive, but consider them "wounded porcupines."

Take the role of a curious researcher. In her constructive use of counseling, Linda began asking herself, "What is Larry doing *for* himself by this action he is doing *to* me?" She began to see the hurts to her as unfortunate by-products of Larry's panicky attempts to arrange meager shreds of security for himself. It helped her not to take personally his embarrassing public remarks to her, when she recognized his primary purpose in making them: to express something about himself, in a way least likely to expose him to ridicule. People typically show nervousness or amusement when men, like Larry, belittle their wives, but they do not ridicule the men.

Curiosity, like compassion, frees us from fear and resentment. When you take the stance of a fascinated onlooker watching the antics that your loved one pulls on you, you open to yourself a whole new way to experience it. As if reading a mystery story, you ask yourself what particular advantage the strong-willed person is after in this instance. Provocative behaviors accomplish several psychological goals for their doers:

1. They evoke intense emotional responses from the victims, reassuring the tormentors that they do indeed

For Better or For Worse
By Lynn Johnston

affect the people who matter to them. Better hated than ignored. At least hated means related.

2. They make other people's actions highly predictable. Strike a man on one cheek and you can bet 99 percent sure that he will strike back at you. Strong-willed adults love the control they feel in making other people respond predictably.

3. They provide evidence to prove the case that provocateurs hold against life: that the people who should love them always give in to impatience instead, and therefore do not merit respect or trust.

4. They reassure the doers that their tactics still work, that they are not pushovers but formidable forces for others to take into account.

Understanding where our loved one is coming from emotionally can help us to feel less degraded by an attack. Seeing the situation through Mom's eyes could have relieved Michael's bewilderment in the last frame of Lynn Johnston's bathtub cartoon.

This chapter has emphasized improvements you can make in a difficult relationship by changes in your own attitude. The next chapter turns to specific actions you can take toward the other person, actions that might make things better between you.

12

Some Things You Can Do

Soft Answers to Wrath

Become smooth. Look at a Velcro fastener under magnification. Notice that one side consists of many tiny hooks and the other side many tiny loops that the hooks can grab. Warm the loopy side enough to melt its irregularities. You get a smooth surface that the hooks cannot grab onto.

Think of your strong-willed loved one's irregular behavior toward you as Velcro hooks reaching out to create with you an unholy bond of abuse and resentment. But see yourself glassy smooth, melted by God's love, so that you have nothing irregular for the hooks to find in you.

To use another example, it takes two persons to sustain a tug-of-war with a rope. The game stops the instant that you drop your end of the rope. No matter how much the other person dangles the rope in front of you, taunts you with it, and teases you to take it, no power struggle goes on when you do not pick up your end of the rope.

Smooth things to say. The following examples represent friendly, noncommittal responses you can give to unkind criticisms, sticky questions, and implications of incompetence on your part from your irregular person.

To criticism:
 1. I'm sorry you feel that way.
 2. Thank you for telling me.
 3. I'll think about that.
 4. You may be right.
 5. Oh. (Can be said with so many tones of voice that it can convey all the following):
    a. I register that you have spoken to me.
    b. I understand. Go on.
    c. I see what you mean.
    d. I'm so sorry to hear that.
    e. Wow! That's interesting. Please tell me more.

To questions:
 6. Good question.
 7. I'm not sure.
 8. I wonder.
 9. I wish I knew.

To either, when the time is right:
10. I must be a terrible disappointment to you.

How to stay smooth. Linda prayed several times a week for her irregular husband, Larry. She did not pray that God would make him easier for her to live with, but that God would find great glory in expressing his own image to the world through the man of God that Larry would someday become. She held in her mind's eye a magnificent vision of Larry as a radiant soldier of Christ, muscular, confident, in the dazzling uniform of an honored officer, wise, kind, gentle, approachable, smiling, humorous, graceful, loyal, a competent leader, respected by his company of dozens of soldiers. In her praying imagination she visualized him tenderly embracing her, and honoring her to bystanders.

This active way of praying took more creative effort from Linda than her former half-hearted, "God bless Larry." It changed her in the direction of alertly looking for the first faint signs of the righteous character that God was already developing in Larry. She became more attuned to the good things about Larry than to the bad things. It sweetened her, and noticeably changed the nature of their interactions.

Linda came to regard her vision of Larry, the man of God, as the real Larry; and the surly guy who stomped around in her life calling himself "Larry" as a kind of comical character who simply happened to be far behind the times. She could chuckle at his antics with the amusing secret between her and God: "Look at that funny guy. He doesn't know who he is yet!"

When Larry made a verbal jab at her, Linda pictured it as a sharp pointed stick onto the end of which she imagined herself sticking a marshmallow, saying privately, "Oh, boy, just what we need for a picnic!" A marshmallow — soft, sweet and nourishing — the opposite of the hard, bitter, poisonous retort that Larry tried to provoke. Linda did not let *his* behavior determine *her* attitude.

Off the wall in the Lord. In this section I want to describe some ideas that I have never seen anyone use, but that I think illustrate the "other cheek" principle in relating to a difficult loved one. Let us continue the above example of Linda and her habitually crude husband, Larry. I think Linda might give some friendly, yet unconventional enough, responses to Larry's discourtesies that she completely removes his payoff and arouses his curiosity instead.

Imagine a social situation in which Larry blurted out, "Linda's so screwy she has to see a shrink every week."

Linda, brimming over with amusement as she saw herself putting a marshmallow on the end of a pointed, shrinking stick, actually bubbled out with the words, "Oh, boy, just what we need for a picnic!" Larry, completely amazed at this non sequitur, stammered, "Wha, what do you mean by *that*?" Linda just grinned, kissed him on the cheek and walked away.

She began using other zany responses whenever he jabbed her, like "geraniums," "two plus two equals four," and the whistled first line of the tune "Happy Birthday." When he demanded to know what she meant by one of these off-the-wall gambits, she never answered verbally. She only smiled, blew him a kiss, and turned away. Larry became increasingly self-conscious about his rude remarks.

Linda, returning good for evil in this unconventional manner, created in Larry's mind a state of beneficial uncertainty. He could not continue his old behavior in the same way as before because Linda no longer played the part that the game required of her. So, Linda could stop Larry from his original destructive game, but she could not program what he would do instead. By her friendly playfulness she increased the odds that he would initiate a more sociable new pattern — but that she left to him. She prepared herself to continue her godly humor, even if he escalated to more savage verbal shots at her.

When Push Comes to Shove

So far, the ideas in this chapter have emphasized the serenity side of wisdom — victims exercising the considerable range of adaptations possible on *their* part to make life with a strong-willed adult more pleasantly workable. But what about the courage side, to boldly work for possible changes in the other person?

True submission means bold reverence. About fifteen years into our marriage, I reached my worst point of strong-willed irresponsibility toward my wife, Ruth. I found fault with her, I avoided doing fun things with her, I spoke abruptly and unkindly to her. Late one evening I sat angrily alone watching TV. Ruth approached me gently, saying, "We need to talk about us. Is now a good time?"

I answered curtly, "I'm busy."

Ruth kindly asked, "When would be a good time for you?"

I spoke louder, "Look. I said I'm busy. Can't you see? I don't want to talk."

Ruth persisted softly. (In those days of strong-willed, midlife insanity on my part, it bothered me that she kept calm, kind, and rational as I escalated my outrageousness. I could have justified my discourtesy more easily if she had shown some toward me.) She said, "We don't have to talk right now, I can wait. But it's essential that we discuss what's been going on with us lately, and I want a definite appointment to do so."

I sprang from my chair, snapped off the TV, turned to Ruth and barked, "Get off my back. Leave me alone. I don't want to talk to you." Then I stomped upstairs into the bedroom, slammed the door, turned off the light, and crawled into bed.

Ruth came up the stairs, threw open the door, clicked on the light, pulled the blankets off of me, sat down on the bed, and looking me square in the eye said sternly, "Our marriage is too important for us not to discuss it. You have never treated me like this before, and we are going to talk about it *now!*"

And I felt loved.

Oh, I kept up a facade of belligerence. And I did feel annoyed at Ruth's persistence. I did not *want* to talk. I did not want to face what I was doing. I was tired, too. So I did not *enjoy* her bold firmness, but it deeply moved me. It stirred in me a secret inner sense of security, to see that the woman to whom I had linked my life cared enough for our partnership to put it above her own petty self-interests, like indulging a vengeful verbal retaliation at me, or sullenly dropping the issue because she found it inconvenient or scary to override my blustering tantrum.

What I proposed was wrong. I abdicated husbandly leadership by refusing to hear my wife's concerns. Therefore, Ruth called me to the responsible action I should have initiated. She submitted herself to God's assignment, not to my whims. She insisted that I do what I had vowed at the wedding altar. By her balanced attitude blending boldness with courtesy toward me, she demanded that I submit not to her wishes but to my own solemn commitments before God.

Regardless of my failure to do my part in our marriage, Ruth did the job that God assigned her. She followed the guidance from the ancient law of God given to Moses: "You shall not oppress *and* wrong one another, but you shall (reverently) fear your God" (Lev. 25:17 AMPLIFIED). She took as her standard for treating me, not my behavior, but God's character. She showed reverence to me as a person made in the image of God — *and exhorted me to act like it!* On another occasion she literally said, "I ask you to act like the man of God you are."

Ruth could not force me to do what I should do, but she could refuse to consent to my irresponsibility.

No contract, no work. Ruth and I ended up with a breakthrough conversation that night that helped us turn a corner for the better in our marriage. But suppose I had not held still for her bold insistence that we talk that night? Suppose I had hit her, or stormed out of the house and stayed away all night, or barred the door to the bedroom, or sat in stony silence, refusing even eye contact with Ruth? What bold follow-up might she have used?

She would not have continued any business as usual until we healed the wound to our marriage covenant represented by my inaccessibility. The minimum essential feature of a mutual relationship is that either can at any time get from the other an agreement to talk about the nature of the relationship. Either one refusing such a request thereby breaches the covenant, leaving discussion and renewal of the covenant the only legitimate business between them. That means Ruth would not prepare meals for me, or run my clothing through the laundry, or even conduct a conversation with me on any other topic until we had resolved to her satisfaction my refusal to discuss our relationship. She would insist on full repentance from me, including what I now considered wrong about what I did, (as described in Chapter 7 of this book, on forgiveness).

Put an end to harassment. Another couple had a conflict the reverse of that between Ruth and me. Rhonda abused her access to Roger by constantly asking him if he loved her and if he had another girlfriend. Her insecurity and jealousy began to suffocate Roger, so he put a stop to it.

He told Rhonda that her demands were pushing him away from her, and that he wanted a solution agreeable to both of them. He proposed one that he had thought out before this conversation. He agreed to answer a maximum of one question per waking hour from her about his love. If she asked more often, he would tell her that he had already answered and she was not to repeat her question until at least sixty minutes from *that* moment. If she asked anyway, he would not answer. If she persisted to a point that Roger considered badgering, he would warn her, "If you ask me one more time in the next hour, I will immediately leave the house, stay elsewhere overnight and return tomorrow at a time of my choosing. When I return, I will tell you I love you, and start over again with the rule that you may not ask me about my love until one hour later." (The day before announcing this proposal, Roger had already packed a bag and arranged a convenient place to stay.)

When Roger asked her how the proposal sounded to her, Rhonda answered, "I only want to know if you love me." Like a typical strong-willed adult, Rhonda thus refused to play a part in setting any rules to govern her behavior. Roger would not let her indecision paralyze him, so he said, "Until I hear a better idea, I will operate by this one starting now."

Refuse hostage status. Always have a Plan B that you can comfortably follow if your undependable partner does not follow through with Plan A that you both agreed upon. Imagine yourself a wife whose husband has vaguely promised to paint the outside of the house. Each time you ask him, "When?" he says, "Don't worry. I'll get around to it." Then he sneers, "What's the matter; don't you trust me?" as if you have some kind of disgusting disease that prompts you to ask for commitments from a loved one on matters that affect you.

Finally, after several weeks in which your husband does nothing about painting the house, you say, "Honey, I have appreciated your willingness to paint the house and, since it's important to me to have it done before cold weather sets in, if your schedule has not allowed you to get around to it by Labor Day, I'll take that as your approval for me to have it done another way." You help him save face by thanking him for his good intentions and implying that only a busy schedule, not a faulty character, would keep him from fulfilling it. Then the day after Labor Day you call a painting contractor to do the job, and do not say a word about it until your husband comes home in a rage to find it done and paid for. Then you calmly remind him that you put him on notice that inaction on his part would constitute a message to you to go ahead without him. The rest of his tantrum you simply tolerate, with occasional soft answers.

Always frame yes/no questions such that nonanswers from the irregular person mean *no*. For example, "Mother, unless you tell me now a definite yes, that you want to go to the play with us, I'm not going to buy you a ticket, and you won't be able to get in."

Strong-willed children of any age love to test you to see what Plan B you have if they do not comply with your threats. The mother in Lynn Johnston's "one-two-three" cartoon had none!

Shall we parent strong-willed adults? No. We use many skills presented in books on child raising, but not to shape the adult's character. Although this rebellious child in an adult's body may, in rare cases, grow up in response to our discipline, we focus on a different goal. We simply arrange that the relationship will function by lawful, orderly principles, or we will not participate in it.

The occasional strong-willed adults who do respond to loving discipline, typically do so dramatically, with tears of deep repentance and a conversionlike change in their lives. They have always wanted someone to care enough to confront.

Solomon in Proverbs 14:7 refers to lawless persons as "fools," and recommends isolating them. That means, to a loved one who attempts to control you by loud-voice intimidation, you say, "I will continue hearing and answering you as long as you honor my signals to lower your voice, slow down, and let me process what you have just said. If you don't slow down when I ask you to, I will walk away." If the fool escalates beyond that point, such as by threatening physical assault, you warn, "If you abuse me, you're no

longer just arguing with a loved one, you are breaking the law, and I will file charges against you."

Then, if you must walk away, you have a Plan B environment already in mind to go to that you really enjoy. One wife had one hundred dollars set aside for such an emergency, with which she treated herself to a luxurious night alone in a hotel room, with a long bubble bath, a delicious box of chocolates, and a bottle of expensive perfume. She made her husband's disrespect for her an occasion for *her* pleasure. She did for herself what he should have done for her, and left him without her for twelve hours.

Jesus lauded a Roman centurion who said, "I, too, am a man under authority." The principles of law and order that you enforce must apply to you. This lets you answer a common move that strong-willed adults employ to justify themselves and disarm you. When you call their behavior abusive and set a limit on it, they say, "You're judging me." They are appealing, of course, to Matthew 7:1 that says, "Do not judge, or you too will be judged." You answer that indeed you are judging them, with full willingness to accept the risk Jesus warned about, namely being judged by the same standard you apply to them.

13

Why You Find It Hard

Nostalgia for Magic

Fred's irregular mother, in her sixties, called him at his office to say she had made some fine potato salad and roast beef that would go to waste unless he came over that night to eat it. He immediately recognized the familiar, unspoken implication in her way of delivering this information. This "music" behind Mom's words meant that, if Fred did not cancel all other plans and rush over to see Mom that night, he must bear the shameful status of an unloving, ungrateful son. He protested that he had already planned with his wife and children to go to their oldest son's Little League game that night.

Mom increased her subtle pressure, shifting into her hurt martyr's tone of voice, and adding an adept bite to her words. "Well, whatever's most important to you, son," she sighed accusingly. "I guess it's hard for young folks like you, surrounded by people who love you, to know what it's like

167

not to have anyone who cares. I worked my fingers to the bone today, fixing a meal that I thought would be appreciated, but, that's okay, I can just throw it out. You do what you have to do. Never mind about me. I'll just watch television . . . alone . . . again."

Fred writhed in agony between feeling angry at Mom's manipulation, and on the other hand feeling guilty for saying *no* to her. What if something happened to her? He could never forgive himself. He had not yet developed a thick skin toward Mom's disapproval. It scared him more than his own family's disappointment over his repeated broken promises.

"Oh, Mom, don't talk that way. I'll see what I can do. Maybe the family won't miss me. Maybe the game will be called on account of rain." Fred always hoped for events to come along and spare him from dilemmas like this current one with Mom.

"I'm *so* glad you can come, Freddie. It hasn't been easy since your father left me. A woman can't move heavy things around, and such. I don't know what I'd do without you. See you at six?" Mom ended.

Fred agreed, hung up, and wandered to the next office. He told the whole story to his friend George, asking urgently, "What should I do?"

Note the absurdity of George giving any advice to Fred. He would be saying, in effect, "I can give, in a fraction of a minute, an answer to a long-standing dilemma that Fred has not solved in dozens of conversations with other persons who urged him to set limits on Mom and endure her tantrums."

Fred, pressing George for an answer, subscribed to magical thinking of his own, with the following unspoken twist: "If I present the desperateness of my situation urgently enough to you, you will divulge to me the splendid answers that you surely possess but would otherwise withhold."

Although Fred might cut his head off for saying this, George would hit the bulls-eye if he would answer sarcastically: "I know exactly what you should do, a wonderful action that I can describe to you clearly and quickly, which you can do instantly and easily, and that will have the immediate effect of permanently transforming your mother's behavior into consistent courtesy and unselfish encouragement. Up until now I have withheld this excellent information from you because I did not care enough about you. But the intensity of your anguish has moved me to the point where I now want to divulge the secret remedy that I always could have told you at any time."

That imaginary response lays bare several strong-willed attitudes in the thinking of persons, like Fred, who refuse to apply bold, reverent tactics to the actions of the strong-willed persons who afflict them:

1. I insist on finding easy answers that work perfectly to enforce my will on the irregular person, without creative effort on my part, nor risk that the irregular person will reject me.
2. Others more capable than I have magic answers that they withhold from me.
3. My most potent input into solving this problem consists of suffering dramatically enough that my pathetic case outrages the sense of fair play on the part of my audience, rousing them to effective remedial actions that spare me the discomfort I do not want to face.

Fred, the agitated man in the above story, does not want to hear any realistic counsel like, "Simply tell your mother pleasantly that you cannot come tonight, but you would like to see her Sunday if okay with her. Let her handle her own disappointment. Don't give in to her manipulations." He hates the thought that Mom might think ill of him for not granting her request. He *demands* that she always think well of him. He loves the effortless myth from childhood fairy tales: "They lived happily ever after."

Reasons You Fail to Act

Laziness. Letting go of the familiar securities of the past and thrusting forward with bold initiatives into the future takes work. Asserting your adult competence requires letting go of your childhood preference for a magical parent to do tough jobs for you.

The more attention you give to viewing your irregular persons as presenting you with overwhelming, insurmountable obstacles, the more you justify your inaction. The worse you make *them* look, the less responsible *you* feel to activate yourself in a bold, godly direction. By exercising the adequacy of adulthood, you jeopardize the secure feelings of childhood, which you maintain by pleading inadequacy. You mask your plea of incompetence by emphasizing the extraordinary difficulty of the problems that your strong-willed adversaries dump on you. Thus you turn the spotlight of potential criticism from yourself and your cowardice, to the culprits and their cruelty.

You may have a vested interest in the scapegoat role. If you continue offering yourself for abuse by your irregular person, you probably still cling to a belief you formulated in childhood: that your family members will not fight with each other if they expend enough anger and hostility toward you. You offer yourself as a shock absorber, so as to feel a little more secure in the belief that the people *whom you think you still need* will stay with you if they get enough relief from their anger at life by taking it out on you. You *volunteer* for the victim role, even though you don't like it. You refuse to sustain your adult self without the supplies that your irregular persons withdraw from you.

In 1974, the United States experienced economic shock as the Oil Producing and Exporting Countries (OPEC) suddenly cut back on the supply of oil, and sharply raised its price. The United States felt the pain of its dependency on OPEC, and decided to become self-sufficient in oil by teamwork among oil companies, governmental agencies, and consumers. When a former supplier became unreliable, we turned to new resources available within us, and worked to develop those. We did not merely settle for making token protests of resentment while keeping a dependency we preferred over effort.

You as an adult no longer need the big people you once relied upon for your psychological supplies. You now have those resources available to you from a team consisting of adult friends, society at large, God's personal presence, and your own experience, diligence, and creativity. Connect your will to them, instead of withdrawing from emotional involvement with reality in your impotent show of resentment toward the parental suppliers on whom you alone choose to keep you dependent.

Stubbornness. "Perhaps the first thing we expect to learn [from any advisor] is how to get the [strong-willed person] to stop [acting irregularly]. This is a difficult idea to pry ourselves loose from, but our 'making it' in [life] depends entirely on realizing that our [irregular person's decency] is not our business, however much it may seem to affect our lives and destroy our happiness" (Adapted from the selection for May 12 in *One Day at a Time in Al-Anon*, 1973).

Where the above quotation for Al-Anon members refers to alcoholism and drinking, the adaptations in brackets refer to strong-willed persons and their irregular behavior. One other quotation from this source (starting off the selection for May 11) fits here, too: "What is the greatest hindrance to my achieving serenity? *Determination* — the grim resolve that I can do *something* about everything." This grimness marks your fight with God, and your rejection of his grace, because grace requires your confession of helplessness.

If you are not applying principles you have learned here and elsewhere on how to live contentedly with a strong-willed, irregular loved one who does not change, you probably have your goal set not on serenity for yourself, but on victory over the other person. You want to make your irregular person tolerable, rather than yourself tolerant. The Institute in Basic Youth Conflicts defines tolerance as "acceptance of others as unique expressions of specific character qualities in varying degrees of maturity" (*Character Clues*, 1974).

The only person who refuses to learn tolerance toward a strong-willed adult is another strong-willed adult.

With her book, *Irregular People* (1982), Joyce Landorf has helped people make sense of difficult relationships they experience. However, both the book and her filmed and tape-recorded remarks on the topic seem to me to carry a tone of unresolved frustration and bitterness. In one sentence Joyce describes her irregular person as "severely handicapped." In the next, she speaks as if he has no handicap. She says, "I've opened up my heart, become vulnerable time and time again, only to feel the terrible pains of rejection! I keep telling myself, 'They *will* see me, they *will* hear me, they have just *got* to. It's abnormal not to see and hear . . . .' But it doesn't happen. The problem goes on and on" (p. 37).

To paraphrase the author, she is saying, "Loved one, I know you have no eyes, but you *must* see me. I realize you have no ears, but I *insist* on you hearing me. I see that you have no arms, but you will be mean and heartless if you do not hug me anyway." She virtually calls her limping loved one to run a brisk ten-minute mile — a worthy task. But to set it before a loved one crippled with congenital palsy simply exposes him to ridicule.

In repeatedly demanding what her irregular person cannot give, Joyce does not accommodate his handicap. She implies that the noble normality of her need ought to nullify the handicapping effect of his handicap. In complaining, "It's abnormal," she means, "My loved one should have come through the holocaust of his own childhood with no scars. I refuse to accept his handicap. I will not digest my own disappointment and breathe a contented 'So be it.' "

Once a man came for counseling about how to handle his strong-willed wife. The counselor gave a number of specific suggestions, like those in this book. The man came back a week later, saying, "I tried it, and it didn't work." He meant that none of it had made his wife act more thoughtfully. The counselor asked in amazement, "It didn't work? You mean you're not a better person?" The man answered peevishly, "That's not what I was after."

". . . out of the overflow of the heart, the mouth speaks," taught Jesus (Matt. 12:34). The man above revealed his heart's preoccupation with outdoing his wife in their power struggles. More than he focused on growing in righteousness as a man of God, he devoted his ardor to defeating his partner.

Pride. Alice has a strong-willed son who refuses to put his dishes in the sink as she requires of him after he eats. She has a strong-willed husband who spends time with a girlfriend and scornfully compares Alice to her. She has a strong-willed father who continues finding fault with her, as he has all her life, calling her "stupid," asking her why she can't be like her older sister, and never admitting that he has ever made a mistake.

Alice fails in the same way with all three of her irregular

persons, and for the same reason. She only thinks about what they *should* do. She acts as if these men in her life lack freedom of choice. When she says, "They should," she refuses to address the question, "What will I do if they don't?" Like the mother in the earlier "One-two-three" cartoon, she has no Plan B.

Alice's blockage reaches deeper than that, however. She regards with revulsion the very notion of designing a Plan B. She reasons that for her to even entertain the idea of "or else" would admit defeat. It would call for her to admit that her men *can* mistreat her.

By not equally planning A and B options, Alice shows that she does not accept *God's* decision to create the men in her life free to do wrong. She attempts to dictate a different design to life than what the Creator himself ordains. She lives in a fantasy world she prefers, one that she created, where the people she loves *cannot* disappoint or disrespect her. She demands the rights of a sovereign. She lives as if *entitled* to the kind of treatment she wants.

What *does* Alice do when her men do not obey? She pursues an unconscious Plan B by default. She sighs, grimaces, rolls her eyes, and slumps her shoulders. These gestures convey retaliatory, punitive messages, calculated to make her irregular men feel guilty, and third parties to feel responsible to take her side. She resorts to rhetorical questions like, "Why can't you ever . . . ?" As with all nagging, she does not expect it to succeed, only to sting the wrongdoer.

In short, by default, Alice does vengeful things when her irregular people mistreat her. And thereby she claims to herself a function of God, who said, "Vengeance is mine."

Strong-willed Alice would be as the Most High. She will stay stuck and bitter and abused until she agrees with God for him to design and maintain his universe as he sees fit, and agrees to take her part in his universe under his jurisdiction. Sanity begins not with self-esteem but with esteem for God.

The Peace We Often Forfeit

Twice a week I notice a woman in high heels walking a dog in our neighborhood. She always walks him the same way — on the edge of disaster. He strains at the leash, pulling her forward at a rate she can just barely maintain without falling on her face.

I ask myself, *Why do she and her dog go at that specific rate? What stops the dog from going faster, so that the lady falls forward? She* stops him, of course. She cannot go any faster without falling, so she imposes a limit on the dog. Since she already sets *some* limit, why does she not set that limit at a lower pace more comfortable for her? The dog is already not going as fast as *he* wants to, so why does she not make him go slower?

With your irregular persons, you already do draw the line somewhere. Why not draw it elsewhere? Perhaps you never thought of it before. Maybe the idea excites you — "*Hey, I do draw the line!*" — and you will relocate it more appropriately. But if you *yes, but* this possibility, you reveal a kind of bent thinking common in our twisted world. It goes like this, a kind of deal with life: "As the intensity of a hardship upon me increases, it eventually reaches a point where it entitles me to refuse anymore. At that point of entitlement I can take whatever action seems fitting to me to protect myself, without incurring criticism."

The twistedness in that line of thinking lies in its works basis, with its reliance on earning and obligation, debit and credit, buying, saving, owing, deserving, and collecting. We impose a market mentality on a grace universe.

The lady dog-walker will firmly heel her dog to a snail's

pace the day she walks with knees bandaged from her fall of the day before. She will think that her injuries give her the right to slow the dog down. Angels could shriek at her from heaven, "You never needed the right; you could have slowed the dog down at any time simply because it made sense to do so." I don't know her, but if she thinks in a strong-willed way, she would thumb her nose at the angels' offer of grace and announce that she prefers the security of believing that she *pays* her way through life.

"Oh, what peace we often forfeit; oh, what needless pain we bear." However, not *just* because we do not carry everything to God in prayer, but because, when we do, we pray amiss. We ask God to ease our conditions. We beg for exemption from the exercise of capabilities he has given us to solve the problems he permits in our lives. We implore him to interfere with natural laws and random occurrences to spare us the pain of normal coping.

We come to peace only when we affirm in our praying that God knows what he's doing in working to correct our mistaken attitudes, rather than to end the painful results of them. Then we pray for the *wisdom* he yearns to give us, to discern the difference between situations we *can* affect and ones we cannot. Exercising this wisdom, we seek his energy to work at the things we can change, and to content ourselves about things we cannot change.

Part Four

Conclusion

14

We Have a Choice

We can reasonably assume that Jesus entered manhood with some aspects of his childhood still undisciplined. Like us, he lived with imperfect parents who surely made mistakes. Yet history does not portray him as a strong-willed adult — childish, stubborn, self-centered. What happened between the time he stopped living under the imperfect authority and discipline of his parents, and the time he entered his public ministry consistently under the authority of the God whom he called "Father"?

At the end of Luke 2 in the Bible, we see Jesus in the temple at age twelve. At the beginning of Luke 4 we find him as an adult undergoing an ordeal of temptation in the desert. The same hot, rocky, barren country that groomed John the Baptist into an effective tool in God's hands, now finds Jesus there, voluntarily, in response to the leading of the Holy Spirit, hungry, under stress.

Choosing Principles for Life

Beliefs, our deepest guiding principles for life, show plainly under stress. Psychologists say that under stress we regress. That is, we fall back on coping mechanisms we developed in early childhood years. We all know the kinds of childish things we do when the usual polite, cooperative ways do not seem to get us what we want. We resort to tantrums, pouting, whining, and helplessness in order to force somebody else to do for us what we ought to do for ourselves. We employ immature, strong-willed maneuvers.

Jesus deliberately put himself into a situation that would tempt him to resort to immature ways. I think he did what we must all do in one way or another in order to become mature. We must consciously choose, by an act of will, our guidelines for living, and whose authority we will respect as ultimate.

Does it strike you, when you think about this story of Jesus in the wilderness, that the people who wrote about it were not there? Jesus alone witnessed these events, then later told the story to his followers. We have in Matthew 4 and Luke 4, the nuggets Jesus considered most significant from his ordeal. He said in one way or another to his disciples, "Of all the struggles I went through out there for forty days, three remain important. My philosophy of life boiled down to three key principles."

Abdicating self-interest. Trying to soften him for the first temptation, Satan approached Jesus on the basis of his *identity.* He said, "If you are the Son of God, tell these stones to become bread" (Matt. 4:3). Brilliant strategy on Satan's part. He realized that part of Jesus' activity out there in the wilderness involved working out his identity. In later years Jesus asked his followers, "Who do *men* say I am? Who do *you* say

I am?" (See Luke 9:18, 20.) In the wilderness he answered the question, "Who do I say I am?"

Satan had a vested interest in sidetracking Jesus from clarifying his identity. So he insinuated that maybe Jesus was not the Son of God: "If you are, then use your power for your comfort."

Jesus wisely did not play into Satan's hands. Had he taken offense at the insinuation, he would have said indignantly, "What do you mean, 'If'? I'll show you! There [zap] some bread!" In trying to show Satan who's boss, he would have unwittingly allowed Satan to be boss. Instead, he stuck to the issue: "Will I make physical comfort a priority for my life?"

Jesus answered, "It is written, 'Man does not live by bread alone, but on every word that comes from the mouth of God'" (Matt. 4:4). He took his stand. Not once, but three times he chose an explicit standard for conducting his life. Each standard came from the written Scriptures of the Hebrew religion — from Deuteronomy.

Jesus chose consciously to abdicate himself as the highest authority in his own life, thus leaving behind him the ways of childhood. He deliberately chose the written Word of God as the authority in his adult life, thus saying, "Rather than live primarily for my own comfort, I will feast on God's teachings about his own character." The bread he hungered for symbolized the physical comforts that we all crave: warmth, relief from pain, money, and the luxuries it can buy.

At times when I have writhed in pain, I thought I would do anything for relief. I used to get carsick as a child and I hated it. I believe if the devil had appeared, even in horns and red costume, and made me an offer, I would have gladly said, "You can burn my soul in hell forever if you'll just get me over this nausea right now."

Jesus chose, as a higher priority for himself: intimacy with the God of the universe, the personal source of all reality.

Accepting natural consequences. Satan came at Jesus a second way. He suggested Jesus throw himself down from a lofty spire of the temple. Here, he appealed to a common wish we all entertain, to evade the natural consequences of our own foolish actions.

I often wish I could read a book while driving a car down the highway at full speed. With that desire I also have the thought that the laws of the universe should bend themselves to accommodate me. The way I reason goes like this: "If God loved me [notice the *if* of doubt, rather than the *since* of faith], he would keep me from harm. He should let me do what I want to do." Something in us wants to rise above natural laws, and hence, above the Lawmaker. We would be as the Most High.

Satan dangled that little morsel in front of Jesus. Jesus answered: ". . . It is written also, 'You shall not tempt, test thoroughly, or try exceedingly the LORD your God' " (Matt. 4:7 AMPLIFIED). He decided he would not engage in foolish actions, expecting God to come and rescue him. That way twists God's arm with blackmail, like, "Hey, God, here's an offer you can't refuse. Either spare me or have your reputation ruined."

People — especially superstitious Christians — often try to coerce God at major decision points in their lives, like getting married. They approach in this way: "Well, I think I ought to marry so-and-so, and if God doesn't want me to, he'll stop me." This implies that if God wants to avoid blame for some future mess in their lives, he must act supernaturally, *now*.

Suppose Jesus had thrown himself off the temple. On the way down, he would be daring God: "Now, if you want the gospel preached in Jerusalem, Judea, Samaria, and the uttermost parts of the earth, you're going to have to cushion me before I hit that hard ground." By such an action, Jesus would have implied that he could take power over God. He would have tried to make the Father bend to the Son's strong will.

But Jesus refused the sin of presumption, declaring (essentially), "Thou shalt not push the Lord thy God into a corner."

Turning down power trips. The third temptation Satan tried on Jesus summarized the other two. He showed Jesus in a glimpse all the political power, control, and influence in the world, and all the real estate, kingdoms, and possessions he could control. Jesus could have everything and everyone under his orders. That sounds very appealing. Think of all the good he could do. He could stop the abuse of power by the Romans. He could legislate morality, eliminate poverty, institute justice. Satan said, "I'll give you all this if you'll just do one small, simple thing — just worship me, by agreeing with my program of taking matters into your own hands."

When I do not acknowledge God as the highest authority in my life, by default I make myself the highest. However, since others have done so before me, I do not initiate the conspiracy of opposition against God's right to rule. In reality I join a movement already underway, initiated long ago and still captained by Satan. This mutiny represents the only alternative to living under God's authority.

If I had killed British soldiers in World War II, I would have helped the German war effort. Even if I murdered for personal reasons, with no loyalty to Adolph Hitler, my action would nonetheless help his political power.

Jesus must have felt a strong tug to go his own way instead of consulting God. He could see himself making the world a better place, like any dictator with world reform ambitions has felt. Why bother to check with God? God would either approve this plan of Jesus', or God would be wrong. Jesus shook off that seductive, poisonous thinking with strong words: "Away from me, Satan! For it is written:

'Worship the LORD your God, and serve him only' " (Matt. 4:10).

The Exercise of Authority

Satan did stop harassing Jesus for a while. Like all strong-willed actions, his tempting attacks came as temporary probes to see who was in charge. Strong-willed children, adults, or devils all have a fascination for authority, which they like to tease, test, challenge, and provoke. They do not know how to exercise authority; only how to oppose it. When they defeat existing authority, they offer none in its place, but only lawlessness, anarchy, and chaos.

Shadows have no substance of their own, but need light to precede them, in order for them to exist by something interfering with the light. In the same way, strong wills offer nothing, they simply oppose. The God who brought order out of chaos said, "Let there be light." Whenever we in our strong-willed tendencies resist God's right to rule according to his light, we nudge the cosmos a step back toward its primordial chaos and darkness. We contribute to the great spoiler's enterprise by joining Satan's rebellion, whether we acknowledge him or not.

Late twentieth-century America is experiencing a gigantic ignorance. We know little about how to live under authority, and even less about how to exercise it. We see one evidence of this defect in the decline of solemnity associated with college and high-school-graduation ceremonies. As one high school official put it, "University graduations have become very unruly at many schools across the country, and high school students see this. There was a change in attitude. Students began to feel that graduation was for them and should be a party. We feel it's for everyone and should be a dignified ceremony that students, parents, and grandparents can remember with pride." (Zorn, E. June 19, 1986, Stompin' grads won't stand on ceremony. *Chicago Tribune*, City/Suburbs Section, p. 6).

Solemnity marks events as different, special, significant in our lives. When we do at commemorative events (like graduations, weddings, convocations, and other ceremonies), the commonplace things we do elsewhere (like telling jokes, and reading magazines), we trivialize those events and fail to punctuate our lives with memorable markers of our transitions. When we adults let kids make of a solemn event just another forgettable party, we contribute to their uncertainty about their role in life. How can children know they have ended one phase of life and moved to a more mature place in society unless someone marks the passage for them by an unforgettable event?

We have a choice regarding authority. We can exercise it and support its exercise over us. Thus we join it as surely as by inhaling and exhaling we join ourselves with the atmosphere that surrounds us. The air itself serves as a physical parable of a spiritual truth. The God who made reality surrounds us by his own authority to do so. And he appoints deputies at many levels to maintain the order that he has instituted.

Strong-willed attitudes oppose authority at all levels and call for strong remedies. The lean, fit, dedicated Israeli army under the command of Joshua supported his authority in obedience to God with these stern words: "Whoever rebels against your word and does not obey your words, whatever you may command them, will be put to death. Only be strong and courageous!" (Josh. 1:18).

What solidarity! How often have you urged a police officer or governing official to be strong and courageous?

Under our present legal system, of course, we adults cannot righteously put to death rowdy teenagers who mock the authority of their school officials. But the attitude of the young toward authority constitutes a life-and-death matter for the nation. It calls for bold, emphatic actions by adults in support of lawfulness that protects the common good. Do not drive over the speed limit yourself nor use a radar-detection device to outwit law enforcement. Destroy any such device that your children use, and refuse them the use of your car for one week following any incident of their traffic-law violation that you observe.

The Book of Judges in the Bible closes with a poignant social commentary: "In those days there was no king in Israel; every man did what was right in his own eyes" (Judg. 21:25 AMPLIFIED). These people continued to revere God in a way as *a* god, the nominal god of the Jews. But they had no heart worship because they did not explicitly choose an external authority to obey, as Jesus did in his wilderness experience. In becoming their own highest authorities, the people turned from the one who called himself the LORD your God, and kept only a god.

Similarly in America today, we hear football coaches referring to "the good Lord" like ancient Greek competitors may have acknowledged good old Zeus, a convenient deity who helps them win their games. We *seek* a god's assistance to us; we *need* a LORD's authority over us.

The End of Immaturity

As kids we all tended to think that the universe revolved around us. The Swiss child psychologist, Jean Piaget, described this normal phase of intellectual development in children. He considered children as budding scientists, coming up with explanations for why things happen as they do. Ask them why it gets dark at night, and they might answer, "To make me go to bed." We all once believed that everything outside of us arranged itself around us, for us, and because of us.

The childish theory actually fits a lot of the facts, especially for first-born children (which Jesus was). Every burp seems like a big deal to the parents. The child mumbles, "Da-da," and the parents think they have an orator in the house. Under stress later in life, we tend to regress and fall back upon this theory as a working hypothesis to make sense of events in our lives, and to guide our actions. We act self-centeredly.

At this point of our vulnerability, Satan mounts a major effort to contaminate God's creation. He cannot keep us from being made in God's image. God already did make us as replicas of his own character, so Satan spitefully does his best to mar that image. He cannot remove our Creator-given creativity, but if he can sidetrack the way we use it, he achieves his purpose. He who cannot prevent us from becoming children of God, seeks to keep us merely children, and to block us from becoming adults of God. He induces us to stay bound up in childish thinking, for Satan works in the realm of our minds. There we wrestle, not against flesh and blood, but against personal powers of spiritual wickedness in dark parts of this world system.

We put childish ways behind us when we acknowledge God as a personal power greater than we are, who preceded us, who created and arranged everything around himself for his own pleasure in a wonderful plan of love, who includes us in that arrangement, and leaves to us the choice of whether or not to join him in his "Plan A." Jesus blazed a trail for us when he chose God's best plan for his human life. He opened to us an alternative to God's "Plan B" death sentence that our original human parents brought upon us by their leadership in the direction of strong-willed opposition to God's authority.

Jesus made three pivotal choices: (1) he would not follow his own will; (2) he would not challenge God's will; (3) he would seek, welcome, and follow God's will — for the joy set before him — regardless of the cost.

We can make those same choices; then say with Paul: "When I was a [strong-willed] child, I talked like a [strong-willed] child, I thought like a [strong-willed] child, I reasoned like a [strong-willed] child. When I became a man, I put [strong-willed] childish ways behind me" (1 Cor. 13:11). "Brothers, I do not consider myself yet to have taken hold of it. But one thing I do: Forgetting what is behind and straining toward what is ahead, I press on toward the goal to win the prize for which God has called me heavenward in Christ Jesus. All of us who are mature should take such a view of things" (Phil. 3:13–15).

For Further Reading

Character Clues (1974). Oak Brook, IL: Institute in Basic Youth Conflicts.

Dobson, J. (1978). *The strong-willed child*. Wheaton, IL: Tyndale.

Dreikurs, R. (1964). *Children: The challenge*. New York: Hawthorn.

Landorf, Joyce (1982). *Irregular people*. Waco, TX: Word Books.

One day at a time in Al-Anon. (1973). New York: Al-Anon Family Group Headquarters, Inc.

Phillips, J. B. (1952). *Your god is too small*. London: Epworth.

Salzman, L. (1968). *The obsessive personality*. New York: Science House.

Smith, Hannah W. (1952). *The Christian's secret of a happy life*. Westwood, NJ: Revell. (Original work published 1870.)

Stapleton, Ruth C. (1976). *The gift of inner healing*. Waco, TX: Word.

Taylor, Dr. and Mrs. Howard (1932). *Hudson Taylor's spiritual secret*. Chicago: Moody Press.